ADVENTISM

Imperiled

ADVENTISM
Imperiled

EDUCATION IN CRISIS

Colin D. Standish
Russell R. Standish

P.O. Box 1, Rapidan, VA 22733

First Edition, October 1984
Typesetting: Flo Smith, Barbara Bohlman, Marquise Knight
Proofreading: Lila Frederick

Second Edition, November 1990
Typesetting: Anne Norris, Ronnie Zmaj, Jackie Locke
Text Layout: Trina Goodwill
Proofreading: Diane Kenaston, Pat Leazer
Managing Editor: Richard J. Bird

Third Edition, August 1998
Typesetting: Rose Heinrich
Design and Layout: Michael Prewitt

Hartland Publications, Rapidan, VA 22733.

ISBN 0-923309-01-2

Scripture quotations marked (NEB) are from *The New English Bible,* The Delegates of the Oxford University Press and The Syndics of the Cambridge University Press, © 1961, 1970. Reprinted by permission.

All Scripture quotations, unless otherwise indicated, are taken from the King James Version.

Contents

SECTION A
God's Educational Paradigm

1. Growing Enlightenment 11
2. Foolishness and Wisdom 13
3. Education and Redemption 19
4. Education and Reformation 25
5. A Balanced Education 33
6. Counterfeit Education 39

SECTION B
Education of the Total Man

7. Physical Education 51
8. Agriculture, the ABC of Education 59
9. Emotional Education 69
10. Social Education 77
11. Intellectual Education 83
12. Spiritual Education 89

SECTION C
Developmental Education

13. Prenatal Education 99
14. The Education of the Infant 105
15. Childhood Education 111
16. The Education of Adolescents 121

SECTION D
Preparation for a Life Calling

17. Home-School Education 129
18. Elementary Education 137
19. Academy and High School Education 143
20. College Education 153

SECTION E
Issues in Contemporary Education

21. Social Relations   163
22. Work Education   171
23. Recreational Education   177
24. Outreach Education   183
25. Dress Education   191
26. What About Accreditation?   199
27. Public Funding of Christian Education   207
28. Academic Freedom in the Adventist School System   213
29. The Education of the Redeemed   223

30. Biography   227

SECTION A

God's Educational Paradigm

Chapter 1
Growing Enlightenment

When, in fifth grade, we had our first experience in a Seventh-day Adventist school, we had little idea of the reason or purpose of Christian education. We knew we'd come from a large public school to a small multigrade school. We realized we now had Bible classes daily. We knew our teachers were members of the Seventh-day Adventist Church, but we knew little of the principles and philosophy of Christian education. Indeed, we became teachers ourselves in Seventh-day Adventist schools without much greater insights, and thus contributed to the offering of a Christian education far short of the pattern that God had entrusted to His people. At this time we had not systematically read any of Ellen White's counsel on education.

In 1965, when Colin was called to head the Education Department at Avondale College, it fell to his lot to teach the course in Philosophy of Christian Education. This of, necessity, required in-depth study of God's educational counsels, opening to him a new vista of the scope and purpose of Christian education. The beauty, logic, and reasonableness of God's way became strikingly evident, together with the conclusion that parents and teachers have often been satisfied with something far short of the best. About this same time, Russell, as the father of a young family reaching towards school age, also intensified his studies of the counsel relevant to the education of his sons.

It was in the middle of the 1970s, however, when it became apparent that the church was facing a gigantic crisis both in theology and in Christian practice. We were led to focus our attention even more specifically upon the educational developments of our church. We have come to the sobering conclusion that the theological crisis in our church is only the symptom, and that the educational practice of the church is the disease. This includes all the educational agencies, the home as well as the school and the church.

This book is not written to place the blame upon anyone or any group, for surely we all stand responsible for what we have fostered or condoned. But it is written to open, before all who will read, the glorious purpose and plan of education that God has exclusively designed for His people. It is the prayer of the authors that the readers will join the rapidly expanding group of Seventh-day Adventists who are committed to having nothing but authentic Christian education for their children, so that they might grow in the knowledge, nurture, and admonition of the Lord, mighty to play their Spirit-filled role in finishing, under the leadership of Christ, the gospel proclamation to the world.

Chapter 2
Foolishness and Wisdom

Paul placed the issues of education within the theater of stark reality when he wrote his first letter to the Corinthian believers.

> For after that in the wisdom of God the world by wisdom knew not God, it pleased God by the foolishness of preaching to save them that believe. For the Jews require a sign, and the Greeks seek after wisdom: but we preach Christ crucified, unto the Jews a stumbling block, and unto the Greeks foolishness; but unto them which are called, both Jews and Greeks, Christ the power of God, and the wisdom of God. Because the foolishness of God is wiser than men; and the weakness of God is stronger than men (1 Corinthians 1:21–25).

> But of Him are ye in Christ Jesus, who of God is made unto us wisdom, and righteousness, and sanctification, and redemption (1 Corinthians 1:30).

> Let no man deceive himself. If any man among you seemeth to be wise in this world, let him become a fool, that he may be wise. For the wisdom of this world is foolishness with God. For it is written, He taketh the wise in their own craftiness (1 Corinthians 3:18, 19).

The world of Paul's day, while dominated by the military prowess of Rome, was still entranced by the culture and education of Greece. Even strict laws failed to stop the elite of Rome from sending their youth to be educated at the feet of the famous Greek teachers and philosophers. Thus Greece still ruled the minds of men. It was not surprising then that Paul's converts in the busy commercial trading center of Corinth had great difficulty drawing away from the concepts of the ultimacy of Greek education. Even the Jewish converts, who had placed such store upon the rabbinical schools, found it hard to adapt to the simplicity of the gospel of Jesus Christ. But Paul, for all his own scholarly training, realized that much of his formal education he would have to unlearn in the school of Christ before he could be the powerful apostle to the Gentiles. For he understood that

The wisdom of this world is foolishness (1 Corinthians 3:19).

In contemporary times we face a situation none too different from that of Paul's day. Many of us have, at least partially, been educated in the schools of the world. We have all too often gained a certain intellectual pride, that we, from humble beginnings and a small distinctive church, have been able to compete more than equally with the scholars of the world. We must confess that we have believed the honored institutions of the world—the Harvards, Oxfords, Heidelbergs—are the standards by which all others, including our own schools and colleges, must be measured. But in so doing we have dishonored God. We have inevitably settled for mediocrity, and we have been a mute witness to the world of our faithlessness and lack of trust in God's way.

The choice is a simple one. We either choose what the world calls wisdom but which God calls foolishness, or we choose what the world views as foolishness but which God calls wisdom. Too often we have chosen the former over the latter.

We must first recognize that there is much truth and much good in secular education. However, it is mixed with subtle errors and it is this fact that makes it dangerous while yet being attractive. Often we forget that the great controversy between Christ and Satan is not the battle between truth and error or good and evil, but the battle between truth and goodness on the one hand and both truth and error and good and evil on the other. The forbidden tree in Eden was the tree of the knowledge of *good* and *evil*. But God gave to our first parents an unadulterated education consisting only of divine truth.

> In His interest for His children, our heavenly Father personally directed their education. Often they were visited by His messengers, the holy angels, and from them received counsel and instruction. Often as they walked in the garden in the cool of the

day they heard the voice of God, and face to face held communion with the Eternal.[1]

Satan ensnared Eve by a mixture of truth and error. The truth was
that she would know much more about evil once she took the step of
disobedience. The error was that she would not die.

> Satan desired to make it appear that this knowledge of good
> mingled with evil would be a blessing, and that in forbidding
> them to take of the fruit of the tree, God was withholding great
> good.[2]

Ever since the first deception Satan has interwoven truth with error
in his effort to deceive man. In one sense he has an enormous advantage
over a "God that cannot lie" (Titus 1:2). For he can employ an infinite
mixture of truth and error in order to deceive and woo. Only those who
know the truth of God's word can perceive his nefarious assaults. But just
as a glass of pure water is poisoned by one drop of strychnine, so the
minutest trace of error destroys the truth of God. Perhaps the most dangerous comment in our church today is, "There's a lot of truth in it." By
clear implication there is also some error, and this fact should alert us
that the message is of Satan.

God allows no compromise with the world. He requires that the children of His people receive an altogether different education from that of
the world—an education fit for a prince or princess of the Kingdom of
Heaven. This education recognizes no teaching that is not founded upon
consistency with the eternal principles of His Word. It recognizes God,
through the Holy Spirit, as the real teacher.

> But the Comforter, which is the Holy Ghost, whom the Father
> will send in My name, He shall teach you all things (John 14:26).

Humanism and secularism are currently invading the educational
systems of the world. Much, especially of humanism, has seemed very
attractive to some Christian educators because of its emphasis upon love
and human worth. But, at its source, it is satanic, for it is man-centered
and not God-centered; and, therefore, it is destined to lead the learner to
lean upon the arm of flesh rather than to develop a simple trusting relationship with God. Humanism ultimately leads to an empty pride in human accomplishment, which, in the end, is destructive of self-worth. True
education acknowledges that there is no goodness in ourselves, but that

God has valued us as of infinite worth. Unlike the empty pride of human accomplishments, which can vary with "success" and "failure," such self-worth is not dependent upon what we can do, but is an acknowledgment of what God has, and is doing, for us through His Son, Jesus.

Whereas most educational systems are built upon materialistic goals such as possessions, property, power, praise, prestige, popularity, and pride, Christian education allows no such egocentric motivation. It is a tragic fact that many Christian parents are firing their children with unholy ambitions, little different from those of the worldling. And, in so doing, they are frustrating the ministry of the Holy Spirit in their children's lives, and are placing them in danger of eternal loss.

The Word of God allows but three valid goals for true education, and it will be noted that none of these is egocentric; rather they are designed to prepare a generation of youth to take up the final challenge to proclaim the love, power, and soon coming of our Lord to a world in desperate need. Such young people will see the glory of the Lord and the salvation of lost humanity as their all-consuming passion.

Aim #1: To give our children and youth a thorough knowledge and understanding of God and His Word. In an age when "darkness shall cover the earth, and gross darkness the people" (Isaiah 60:2), the glory of God's truth needs to be in the minds and hearts of His people. The primacy of implanting the Word of God in the mind is emphasized by Paul.

> So then faith cometh by hearing, and hearing by the word of God (Romans 10:17).

There can be no thorough work of conversion in the life, unless there is a knowledge of the true character of our God and a clear understanding of His messages to mankind.

Aim #2 : To lead our children and youth to the complete surrender of their lives to the will of Jesus.

We cannot force one soul to surrender to Christ because the very nature of surrender requires a volitional choice. Force is inimical to the love of God. However, it is the privilege of every parent and teacher to make the claims of Christ upon the lives of the children as attractive and meaningful as possible. Thus Paul counsels:

> Ye fathers, provoke not your children to wrath: but bring them up in the nurture and admonition of the Lord (Ephesians 6:4).

Aim #3: To educate our children and youth in service to God and man.

Once the love of God is received into the life, that love cries out for expression. Christian growth is predicated upon a meaningful prayer life, a continuing study of God's Word, and the witness of the message of God in words and deeds. The newly-received Christian experience of the youth will soon wither and die if the avenue of expression is not made possible. The Christian is born for servanthood. How much care should be given to the daily training of our youths in service as we aim to see them participate in the greatest and most significant venture ever entrusted to man!

What God said concerning ancient Israel is true even more so at the end of probationary time.

> Ye are My witnesses, saith the LORD, and My servant whom I have chosen: that ye may know and believe Me, and understand that I am He: before Me there was no God formed, neither shall there be after Me (Isaiah 43:10).

> I have declared, and have saved, and I have shewed, when there was no strange god among you: therefore ye are My witnesses, saith the LORD, that I am God (Isaiah 43:12).

To this point of human history, Satan has had unfailing success in corrupting God-centered education. This has required God to raise up successive generations of His children to begin according to His plan. The vast education program of the Seventh-day Adventist Church did not accidentally commence but was designed to prepare a people for the fellowship of holy beings in Heaven. Satan's deceptive assaults have been witnessed at every level. He realizes the danger, to his cause, of youths educated according to God's plan. Thus, in 1894, God gave the following warning:

> Our institutions of learning may swing into worldly conformity. Step by step they may advance to the world; but they are prisoners of hope, and God will correct and enlighten them, and bring them back to their upright position of distinction from the world.[3]

Two years later, the warning was more explicit. Already Satan had worked his web of worldliness into our schools.

Though in many respects our institutions of learning have swung into worldly conformity, though step by step they have advanced toward the world, they are prisoners of hope. Fate has not so woven its meshes about their workings that they need to remain helpless and in uncertainty. If they will listen to His voice and follow in His ways, God will correct and enlighten them, and bring them back to their upright position of distinction from the world.[4]

We dare not be obscurants claiming our education is continuing according to God's order. To do so would be to second the destructive work of Satan. While the restoration of the home and school is God's work, God is not a manipulator, and will never function against man's choice. Thus the hope of Seventh-day Adventist education is indeed the preparation of a generation which will demonstrate to the world the love, mercy, power, and be ready for the soon coming of Jesus. This belief is postulated upon our fulfilling the following vital conditions.

If they will listen to His voice and follow in His ways, God will correct and enlighten them, and bring them back to their upright position of distinction from the world.[5]

Thus this volume is dedicated to the discovery of an educational program which is exclusively designed for the children of light. It is the education that God has provided for the salvation of His people, and for the enlightenment of the world.

1. White, Ellen G., *Education*, page 21.
2. Ibid., page 24.
3. White, *Fundamentals of Christian Education*, page 290.
4. White, *Testimonies for the Church*, Volume 6, page 145.
5. Ibid., italics supplied.

Chapter 3
Education and Redemption

When we arrived at Avondale College as immature 16-year-olds, in 1950, our vocational options were scanty. Basically the college offered courses in secretarial science, accounting, building construction, teaching, and ministry. None of the first three appealed to us, and we selected teaching because we knew that we were not "good enough" to be ministers. How limited was our understanding then of the sacredness of the high calling of those who wish to be the educators of the children of God's people!

One of the most striking statements concerning education made by Ellen White is her declaration:

> In the highest sense, the work of education and the work of redemption are one.[1]

This statement forces the Christian to reevaluate all his cherished definitions of education. It translates educational aims out of the confines of the immediate into the realm of eternal verities. This truth does not mean that Christian education has nothing to offer for the immediate, for to place education in the realm of the eternal is indeed to greatly enhance the meaning and significance of that which is taking place in the present. This truth does, however, reduce progressive-humanistic and social-reconstruction concepts of education to the realm of the redundant—totally inadequate for the education of the child of God.

Colin once had a professor who, after detailing a sampling of the various definitions of education, claimed that, in presenting his own definition, he was giving the broadest definition possible. He then defined education as "the total experience of man from conception to death." This definition pointedly illustrates the limitations of secular concepts of education. How vastly greater in its scope is God-centered education!

> Our ideas of education take too narrow and too low a range. There is need of a broader scope, a higher aim. True education means more than the pursual of a certain course of study. It means more than a preparation for the life that now is. It has to do with the whole being, and with the whole period of existence possible to man. It is the harmonious development of the physical, the mental, and the spiritual powers. It prepares the student for the joy of service in this world, and for the higher joy of wider service in the world to come.[2]

Seventh-day Adventists are among the most educationally conscious group in society and this is right. We believe that the talents entrusted to us are gifts from God to be used and multiplied. Yet we must ever be reminded that they are to be used for His glory and for a witness to mankind. It is thus not surprising that most Adventists, or their forebears, accepted the Advent faith while in humble circumstances. Today the members of the Seventh-day Adventist Church stand high in social status and educational achievement. Thus there is a danger of regressing to worldly evaluation of education. We have sometimes been guilty of worshiping at the altar of the degree, and have seen this goal as the ultimate of higher education. But God allows no such definition.

> Higher education is an experimental knowledge of the plan of salvation, and this knowledge is secured by earnest and diligent study of the Scriptures. Such an education will renew the mind and transform the character, restoring the image of God in the soul. It will fortify the mind against the deceptive whisperings of the adversary, and enable us to understand the voice of God. It will teach the learner to become a co-worker with Jesus Christ, to dispel the moral darkness about him, and bring light and knowledge to men. It is the simplicity of true godliness our passport from the preparatory school of earth to the higher school above.

> There is no education to be gained higher than that given to the early disciples, and which is revealed to us through the word of God. To gain the higher education means to follow this word implicitly; it means to walk in the footsteps of Christ, to practice

His virtues. It means to give up selfishness, and to devote the life to the service of God. Higher education calls for something greater, something more divine, than the knowledge to be obtained merely from books. It means a personal, experimental knowledge of Christ; it means emancipation from ideas, from habits and practices, that have been gained in the school of the prince of darkness, and which are opposed to loyalty to God. It means to overcome stubbornness, pride, selfishness, worldly ambition, and unbelief. It is the message of deliverance from sin.[3]

Such a definition means that higher education is not limited to any age group or any prescribed academic level. It is the education that must be given to the babe in his mother's arms; to the preschool child as he works with his parents and as he learns at their knees; to the elementary school child as he masters not only the skills of formal education but learns also of the One who is the source of all wisdom and true knowledge; to the high-school pupil who seeks to discover God's unique calling in his life; to the college student as he earnestly makes special preparation for his life calling; to the married adults as they allow Christ to establish a home where the pure principles of Christian love prevail; to the middle-aged as they seek to channel their experience into avenues of more fruitful ministries; and to the aged as they utilize their retiring years for their ministry of faith and love. Indeed this will be the education that will be our privilege to enjoy throughout eternity.

Some years ago the Power Coaching College of Sydney, Australia, used as its slogan *Knowledge is Power.* But such an unqualified slogan is hardly acceptable to the Christian in the light of Eden, where additional knowledge brought terrible impotency to earth's first inhabitants. At the turn of the century the well-known British educator, Findlay, proclaimed, *Knowledge is power when it is used.* While an improvement, even this definition is inadequate; for we have seen that the knowledge of drugs and certain lifestyles lead to the ruination of many of our fellow humans. Ellen White, however, places the issue in the spiritual sphere:

Knowledge is power, when united with true piety.[5]

Only the true Christian can discern truth, discriminate between useless knowledge and knowledge of real value, and understand how to translate that knowledge into the principles of righteousness and service. Only the committed Christian is taught by the true Teacher—the Holy Spirit.

> But the Comforter, which is the Holy Ghost, whom the Father will send in My name, He shall teach you all things, and bring all things to your remembrance, whatsoever I have said unto you (John 14:26).

True education elicits a motivation that turns away from man's achievement to the glory of God.[6]

> Let your light so shine before men, that they may see your good works, and glorify your Father which is in heaven (Matthew 5:16).

> Herein is My Father glorified, that ye bear much fruit; so shall ye be My disciples (John 15:8).

> Let all your behavior be such as even pagans can recognize as good, and then, whereas they malign you as criminals now, they will come to see for themselves that you live good lives, and will give glory to God on the day when he comes to hold assize (1 Peter 2:12, NEB).

> Be ambitious, for the Master's glory.[7]

Therefore, the Christian seeks an education for himself and his children of a *different* order from that of the world. The goals are *different;* the teachers are *different;* the curriculum is *different;* methodology is *different;* the context is *different;* and, therefore, the product is *different.*

> True education is the inculcation of those ideas that will impress the mind and heart with the knowledge of God the Creator and Jesus Christ the Redeemer. Such an education will renew the mind and transform the character. It will strengthen and fortify the mind against the deceptive whisperings of the adversary of souls, and enable us to understand the voice of God. It will fit the learned to become a co-worker with Christ.[8]

> It is the privilege of every student to take the life and teachings of Christ as his daily study. Christian education means the acceptance, in sentiment and principle, of the teachings of the Saviour. It includes a daily, conscientious walking in the footsteps of Christ, who consented to come to the world in the form of humanity, that He might give to the human race a power that they could

gain by no other means. What was that power? The power to take the teachings of Christ and follow them to the letter.[9]

The life on earth is the beginning of the life in heaven; education on earth is an initiation into the principles of heaven; the lifework here is a training for the lifework there. What we now are, in character and holy service, is the sure foreshadowing of what we shall be.[10]

The true higher education is what makes students acquainted with God and His word, and fits them for eternal life.[11]

It will be seen that the development of character is the most essential object of education, for by this is determined the understanding of every great choice in life—from a life calling to a life partner. Indeed, upon the character hinges the eternal destiny of every human soul. Thus God's education lifts man from the lowlands of his own imprisoning egocentricity to the highlands of developing and using his talents to serve God and his fellowmen. A life of usefulness is inevitably a fulfilled life.

If students are led to understand that the object of their creation is to honor God and to bless their fellow men; if they recognize the tender love which the Father in heaven has manifested toward them, and the high destiny for which the discipline of this life is to prepare them,—the dignity and honor of becoming the sons of God,—thousands will turn from the low and selfish aims and the frivolous pleasures which have hitherto engrossed them.[12]

To bring man back into harmony with God, so to elevate and ennoble his moral nature that he may again reflect the image of the Creator, is the great purpose of all the education and discipline of life.[13]

Therefore, Christian education requires a revival of the initial education given to man.

Under changed conditions, true education is still conformed to the Creator's plan, the plan of the Eden school.[14]

The great principles of education are unchanged. "They stand fast forever and ever," for they are the principles of the character of God.[15]

23

Such an education is perfectly calculated to prepare a people to proclaim the everlasting gospel to every corner of the earth, and to educate a people who will inhabit God's eternal kingdom.

1. White, *Education,* page 30.
2. Ibid., page 13.
3. White, *Counsels to Parents, Teachers, and Students,* page 11.
4. Ibid., pages 11, 12.
5. White, *Testimonies for the Church,* Volume 4, page 427.
6. See chapter entitled, "Foolishness and Wisdom."
7. White, *Messages to Young People,* page 100.
8. White, *Fundamentals of Christian Education,* page 543.
9. White, *Counsels to Parents, Teachers, and Students,* page 36.
10. White, *Education,* page 307.
11. White, *Fundamentals of Christian Education,* page 431.
12. White, *Counsels to Parents, Teachers, and Students,* page 21.
13. Ibid., page 49.
14. White, *Education,* page 30.
15. Ibid.

Chapter 4
Education and Reformation

The Greeks believed knowledge was equated with virtue—to know was to do. Strange though this concept might seem, it persisted strongly into the nineteenth century when it was confidently predicted that all the social ills of poverty, mental illness, corruption, crime, and war would be eliminated by universal education. We have witnessed the complete collapse of this philosophy.

Education, fully conceived, is not limited to formal schooling but involves the whole experience of man, earthly and eternal. It is both life and preparation for life. There has always been an inseparable link between the extension of the frontiers of God's church and education—not an education imprisoned by the philosophy of man but an education vitalized by the eternal verities of God. Every great religious movement has reawakened and redirected the educational vision of man.

It was always God's plan that man should expand his knowledge, understanding, and wisdom. Though man was created perfect, his understanding was to continuously develop. This was the opportunity to learn, not the unstable theories and hypotheses of today, but the immutables of God. God Himself was man's first teacher.[1]

In the Fall of man is witnessed the introduction of pseudoeducation, the intermingling of truth with error.[2] Subsequently, the world has witnessed the presence of both the true and the false. Very often the two have merged, to the inevitable weakening of the work of the church.

Originally, God entrusted the education of the children to their parents,[3] particularly to the father, the patriarch of the family. And today in a special sense, the responsibilities in education are those of the parents.[4] In ancient times, the father was the teacher, priest, and legislator, and had he faithfully fulfilled his mission, the great truth of God would have been witnessed to the world of antiquity. But when apostasy and idolatry became widespread throughout Israel, God established, through His prophet, Samuel, the schools of the prophets. These were schools which taught the law of Moses, poetry, sacred music, and religious history. The pupils supported themselves by working in the fields and forests. For centuries the schools of the prophets were the only bastion against the widespreading apostasy.

With the restoration of Jerusalem and the return of the Jews to Judah, a new educational system arose that was dedicated to the training of the children for God as a protection against idolatry. Synagogues and rabbinical schools predominated. Such was the emphasis of God's people upon education that it has been stated:

Of all the ancient peoples of the Western World, the Jews were the most literate—the only people of antiquity to attempt to teach everyone to read.[5]

Neither was Jewish education confined to intellectual development. The duty of every father was to teach his son a trade.[6]

For a time, the truth of God was expounded with great care, but later the influence of the Greek culture led to emphasis upon scholarship, philosophy, and religious form rather than upon personal consecration.

It was into this world that the Son of God was born—the great Teacher of humanity. The message of salvation and hope that Christ brought to the world was characterized by the direct, simple methods of the Master Teacher. His teaching was in marked contrast to the abstruse philosophies of the rabbis, Pharisees, and Sadducees.

Yet there are many evidences of the great impact that the teachings of Christ had upon His hearers. As a lad of 12, He astonished the rabbis with His understanding and answers.[7] During His ministry, Christ's teaching impressed and amazed His hearers. The great Nicodemus, a ruler of the Jews and member of the Sanhedrin, could declare, "Rabbi, we know that thou art a teacher come from God" (John 3:2).

As Christ taught in the synagogues, many of the listeners marveled at His knowledge[8] and "wondered at the gracious words which proceeded out of his mouth" (Luke 4:22).

Even when officers were sent to take Him prisoner, they returned without Christ, declaring, "Never man spake like this man" (John 7:46).

As Jesus completed His earthly ministry, He challenged His followers to teach all nations.[9] Thus a new band of teachers arose, taught and trained by the Son of God, fired by a worldwide mission and a fervent belief in the gospel of salvation they were preaching. Within a few short decades the teachings of Christ were proclaimed to the major known regions of the earth; and for the first time in history the message of truth penetrated, with striking success, the heathen cultures of the world.

Christianity expressed new concepts in education. Long had the education of the mind dominated the educational theories of man. But Christianity gave a new zest to the notions of a balanced education—one in which the education of the mind was but part of the total education of man, where both spiritual and physical experiences of man were also given proper education.

Soon arose the first Christian school. Some suggest that it is possible that these arose during apostolic times.[10] Certainly, in the years immediately following the time of the apostles, many of these arose. While their organization was informal and their methods of instruction varied, they were responsible for teaching Christian beliefs to many who were preparing for baptism.

However, just as the Greek influence had penetrated the rabbinical schools of the pre-Christian Jews, so it eroded the purity of the Christian church. Soon catechistic, monastic, and cathedral schools were established; many of these influenced, not only by the Greeks but also the pagan religions of the Romans and Persians. These schools, rather than being the fortresses of truth, became centers for the dissemination of corrupted faith. It is true that, in the West many of the Roman Church leaders such as Tertullian (155–222), Jerome (340–420), and Augustine of Hippo (354–430) spoke out strongly against this trend. But paganism continued to make progress within the dogma of the Christian church.

During this period of growing apostasy, the strongest resistance to the growth of Christian declension was found in the schools of the British Isles. Almost as soon as Christianity was taken across the Channel, either in apostolic or immediate postapostolic times, schools were attached to the established churches.

The schools were annexed to, or rather were part of, the foundation of the churches.[11]

Later two great centers of Celtic learning were established. The first was established by Columba (521–597) on the Island of Iona, off the west coast of Scotland. Here was an education based upon the study of the Word of God and supported by the agricultural work of those who attended. A little later, Oswald (605–641), King of Northumbria, a former pupil at Iona, founded the second great Celtic school at Lindisfarne. Both of these schools, for centuries, stood strongly against the encroachment of apostate Christianity. Though, as a result of the Council of Whitby in 664, much of England accepted papal authority. The Celtic church, particularly in Scotland, remained apart for five more centuries. From the time of Columba until the thirteenth century, Celtic education was said to be remarkable for its vigor and culture, making it perhaps the most outstanding of all Europe.[12]

On the continent, the primitive apostolic faith was maintained over many centuries by the people of the Piedmont valleys. The Waldensians, as they later became known, resisted the great apostasy that swept most of Christendom, clinging to the Bible as their only source of belief. Great and bloody was the persecution that they experienced from the established church. Assailed by such bitter opposition, the training and education of their children was very precious to the Waldensians.

> From earliest childhood the youth were instructed in the Scriptures, and taught to regard sacredly the claims of the law of God. Copies of the Bible were rare; therefore its precious words were committed to memory. Many were able to repeat large portions of both the Old and the New Testament. . . . They were educated from childhood to endure hardness, to submit to control, and yet to think and act for themselves.[13]

It was this education which enabled many of the young men of the valley to carry out their missionary work at great risk to themselves.

When the Reformation of the sixteenth and seventeenth centuries recaptured the spirit of the Bible-centered Christianity, there were whole new implications for education. Luther had emphasized the "priesthood of all believers"; he had stressed that salvation was a personal matter, that neither priest nor prelate had authority over the personal convictions of the individual. Yet if all were to be individually responsible for their salvation, and personal faith was to be derived from a study of the Word, then all must learn to read." Thus the principle of universal education, which perhaps only the Jews in past history had achieved, became a dynamic concern of the Reformation. Further, new impetus was given to the study of the vernacular, which had suffered because of the previous emphasis upon the classics. Protestant education tended to broaden the curriculum, uplift the vernacular, and push toward universal education. It is understandable that

> Luther did not concern himself about the education of the clergy only; it was his desire that knowledge should not be confined to the church; he proposed extending it to the laity who hitherto had been deprived of it.[14]

Luther desired freedom for education; a freedom "indifferent, like the gospel, to distinctions of sex or social class."[15] Thus education was of a twofold purpose—to allow for the enlightenment of the common people as well as the elite, and to propagate throughout Christendom the knowledge necessary for a profound study of the holy Scriptures.[16]

However, because of his heavy responsibilities in proclaiming his message of liberty, Luther was unable to devote his full efforts to the implementation of his educational aims. To a large extent this was the task of Luther's close friend and confidant, Melanchthon. The greatest impetus to education arose, however, out of the Swiss Reformation led by John Calvin. Early in his work Calvin realized that "The word of God is indeed the foundation of all learning."[17]

Therefore much effort was expended in establishing schools and colleges. The influences of Calvin were witnessed, not only in the schools of Switzerland, but also in many other regions. The Huguenots of France, the Protestants of Holland, the nonconformists of England, the Presbyterians of Scotland, were all greatly influenced. Further, the Puritans took Calvinistic principles with them to the New World, and great institutions such as Harvard were originally founded upon this.

In many ways the Scottish educational system, under the dynamic leadership of Calvin's disciple, John Knox (1502–1572), achieved the highest standard of education. Knox devised a plan that allowed for education at all levels from primary through university, providing opportunity for all children to have at least some education. By comparison, in England the education of the day was very confined. Only the outlawed nonconformist schools, often operating secretly, could compare in standard and quality.

The last of the great Protestant reformers to stimulate educational revival was John Comenius (1592–1670). Comenius was the last of the bishops of the Moravian Brethren, a devout group located mainly in Czechoslovakia and later also in the United States. The influence of Comenius, though not great in his own day, became the basis of the great child-centered movements of the eighteenth and nineteenth centuries led by Pestalozzi, Froebel, and Herbart. These movements revolutionized the education of children, especially younger ones.

It is not by chance that education is so central to the Seventhday Adventist Church. Indeed the church could not be the avenue through which Christ presents the last great reformation movement to the world, by which the character of God will be revealed to its inhabitants, unless it had a God-centered education.

The training and education of children has always been a most sacred trust committed to God's people. It is not surprising, then, that every great revival has stimulated the progress of education, and has sought to reestablish education within the fuller context of redemption. In a world that's largely influenced by secular trends, it is essential that Seventh-day Adventists give primary place in education to the values of eternal consequence. There is a need to buttress the three R's with the fourth R (religion), not merely as an addition to the curriculum, but as a principle pervading the curriculum and the methods of teaching. It is to this end that Seventh-day Adventist colleges and schools have been established. They are to offer an education in the tradition of those educational systems of the past which have sought first the kingdom of heaven. Their graduates are to honor the schools' objectives by delivering the gospel to every continent of the earth.

1. Genesis 1:27–30; 2:16, 17.
2. Genesis 3:1–7.
3. Deuteronomy 6:6–8.
4. Ephesians 6:4.
5. Atkinson, C.; Maleska, E. T.; *The Story of Education,* (Bantam Books, Inc., ©1962), page 14.
6. Ibid., page. 17.
7. Luke 2:46, 47.
8. Matthew 13:55; Mark 6:2, 3.
9. Matthew 28:19.
10. Cole, P. R., *A History of Educational Thought,* (Oxford Press, ©1937), page 19.
11. Curtis, S. J., *History of Education in Great Britain,* (University Tutorial Press Ltd., ©1963), page 3.
12. It is incredible to the twentieth-century mind to learn that ignorance was so much a part of the papal system that there were renowned English kings in this period who were illiterate. This situation well-served the Catholic principle of clerical dominance.
13. White, *The Great Controversy,* page 67.

14. D'Aubigné, J. H., *History of the Reformation of the Sixteenth Century,* (Robert Carter & Bros., ©1881), page 376.
15. Boyd, W., *The History of Western Education,* (Adam & Charles Black, ©1947), page 189.
16. D'Aubigné, page 375.
17. Boyd, page 198.

Chapter 5
A Balanced Education

B alance is a concept with unique connotations to non-Christian religions. It is especially evident in Hinduism, Buddhism, Zoroastrianism, Shintoism, and Taoism. This balance is symbolized by the cross, the swastika, the star of David, and the yin and the yang, which are prolific, wherever these religions are practiced. The whole basis of these religions is the balancing of the cosmic opposites in the universe, e.g., light and dark, male and female, height and depth, good and evil. It is the concept of the pagans that these opposites must be kept in cosmic balance. This philosophy therefore demands good gods and evil gods, male and female gods, hermaphrodite gods, and male and female priests. One of the pagan's great challenges is to sufficiently ingratiate himself to the good gods so as to receive all their blessings and benefits, while sufficiently appeasing the bad gods so that he avoids their curses and negative manifestations.

What a contrast we find in Christianity! We know a God who is all-loving and merciful, who is long-suffering even to those who are in rebellion against Him. Thus the balance we look for in Christian education is in stark contrast with the pagan concepts. This balance does not seek to harmonize two impossible opposites, but brings the God-given elements of human existence into one pulsation of harmony. Education in which the provision for this harmonious development is not found, is spurious education.

Ellen White frequently deals with the threefold education of God's children—physical, intellectual, and spiritual.

[True education] is the harmonious development of the physical, the mental, and the spiritual powers.[1]

Wherever we turn, in the physical, the mental, or the spiritual realm; in whatever we behold, apart from the blight of sin, [the knowledge of God] is revealed. . . . The mind of man is brought into communion with the mind of God, the finite with the Infinite. The effect of such communion on body and mind and soul is beyond estimate.[2]

When Adam came from the Creator's hand, he bore, in his physical, mental, and spiritual nature, a likeness to his Maker.[3]

To restore in man the image of his Maker, to bring him back to the perfection in which he was created, to promote the development of body, mind, and soul, that the divine purpose in his creation might be realized—this was to be the work of redemption. This is the object of education, the great object of life.[4]

Useful occupation was appointed [Adam and Eve] as a blessing, to strengthen the body, to expand the mind, and to develop the character.[5]

It is interesting to note that Ellen White consistently commences with the physical education and ends with the spiritual. This approach brings forth a number of insights. In our earthly pilgrimage we become a physical organism at conception; but time is needed before our intellectual processes begin to function. Our nervous system must be sufficiently developed to allow us to begin to monitor our environment. Perhaps the miracle is how quickly our nervous system develops in our prenatal state. The development of our intellect is necessary before we can begin to know our God and to experience the call of the Holy Spirit upon our lives. It is through the physical needs that so often the truth of God finds access to the minds of men and leads them to make a decision for or against their heavenly Father.

The purpose of Christian education is to maximize the healthy growth of the total man. Thus God-centered education provides an education which carefully nurtures the development of the body, the mind, and the soul. For centuries man considered the development of the mind as the focus of education. More recently, education has been expanded to include the physical, but God's educational program is not complete until the spiritual dimension is carefully nurtured. Indeed, the spiritual education becomes the center around which all other education revolves.

We must hasten to add that Satan has a counterfeit to God's balanced education. Concepts of wholistic (holistic) education are proliferating with great rapidity. But such education is usually Satan's counterfeit.

Counterfeit 1—The Physical
   a. Competitive games and sports
   b. The martial arts of the East
   c. The spiritualistic exercises of the East (i.e. yoga)

Counterfeit 2—The Intellectual
   a. Humanistic principles
   b. Mind-control programs
   c. Hypnotic and biofeedback training
   d. Encounter and sensitivity groups

Counterfeit 3—The Spiritual
   a. Esthetic training
   b. Eastern meditation
   c. Mysticism and spiritism
   d. The charismatic movement

What then is the authentic physical, intellectual, and spiritual education that God provides for His children? The education God gave to unfallen man in the Garden of Eden is the basis of education for the children of light today.

> The system of education instituted at the beginning of the world was to be a model for man throughout all aftertime.[6]

> Under changed conditions, true education is still conformed to the Creator's plan, the plan of the Eden school.[7]

Thus from the story of Eden we can gain a clear insight into the education that will be fit for those who will inherit the kingdom of God. The foundation of fulfilling physical education is to be found in the horticultural work provided for Edenic man.

> And the LORD God took the man, and put him into the garden of
> Eden to dress it and to keep it (Genesis 2:15).

The basis of physical development has always been useful manual labor, with a special emphasis upon agriculture. Today we have a diminished interest in agriculture as an occupation, due largely to the massive consolidation of properties precipitated by mechanization. Yet there is a growing movement away from the cities. However, agricultural education is valuable also for physical development.

> Useful occupation was appointed them as a blessing, to strengthen
> the body, to expand the mind, and to develop the character.[8]

It is notable that God-planned education has always been centered upon useful and productive labor, never upon sports or amusements. This was true in the schools of the prophets; it was true in the post-exilic schools of Judah. The useful-labor program does not deny the vital place of other forms of noncompetitive recreation. There is a need for a change of pace and location every now and again, for such natural recreation will enhance the spiritual ministry of the participants.

The intellectual training of the dwellers in Eden was indeed highly scientific. What a wonder to learn the great truths of the universe from the Creator Himself! There was no need for theories or hypotheses; no necessity to speculate, for the Author of science was their Teacher. We can deduce from Inspiration that our first parents at least studied botany, geology, astronomy, earth sciences, oceanography, zoology, and physics.

> The book of nature, which spread its living lessons before them,
> afforded an exhaustless source of instruction and delight. On
> every leaf of the forest and stone of the mountains, in every shin-
> ing star, in earth and sea and sky, God's name was written. With
> both the animate and the inanimate creation—with leaf and
> flower and tree, and with every living creature, from the levia-
> than of the waters to the mote in the sunbeam—the dwellers in
> Eden held converse, gathering from each the secrets of its life.
> God's glory in the heavens, the innumerable worlds in their or-
> derly revolutions, "the balancings, of the clouds" (Job 37:16), the
> mysteries of light and sound, of day and night—all were objects
> of study by the pupils of earth's first school.[9]

Above all, the center of this education was a knowledge of God, of His character of love, and of His greatness and power. Not only did the spiritual life of Adam and Eve center upon direct communion with Jesus and the angels; but God also recognized that a special day for spiritual renewal was essential for man's upward progress.

> And God blessed the seventh day, and sanctified it (Genesis 2:3).

While today we no longer have direct face-to-face communion with our God, we do have a revelation of Him in the sacred Scripture. In its study, we have the same opportunity for spiritual growth in the pathway of Christ-likeness. When Adam came from the hand of the Creator, he was perfect, but immature.

> When Adam came from the Creator's hand, he bore, in his physical, mental, and spiritual nature, a likeness to his Maker. "God created man in His own image" (Genesis 1:27), and it was His purpose that the longer man lived, the more fully he should reveal this image—the more fully reflect the glory of the Creator. All his faculties were capable of development; their capacity and vigor were continually to increase.[10]

In like manner, when we receive the perfection of Christ, we are most immature children; but, as we grow in sanctification we "advance from one stage of perfection to another."[11]

Thus translating the principles of a balanced education into the education and training of our children, parents and teachers must intelligently and purposefully design daily programs, from the earliest years, for children and youth to expand and develop their physical, intellectual, and spiritual resources. These programs will commence with the modeling of God's program of physical, intellectual, and spiritual development in the lives of parents and teachers. Children are master mimics, and are far more likely to follow what we do than what we teach. They need to witness daily the fulfillment of a God-given lifestyle. This example is in such contrast to the world that parents and teachers will have to redouble their efforts for it to be effective in the child's life. As soon as possible, the child's understanding of the benefits of such a lifestyle should be intelligently and attractively fostered.

A balanced education should be a lifetime commitment; for each facet of man, when continually strengthened, enhances the others. A strong physical constitution strengthens intellectual and spiritual powers of growth and service. An actively expanding mind allows more intelligent approaches to physical development and spiritual ministry. A deep daily communion with God obtains the power for victory in the physical sphere and a profitable direction in intellectual expansion.

Careful planning is needed so that our children can daily learn practical physical skills, particularly in the out-of-doors, where they are encouraged to study lessons that reflect the God-centered knowledge of our world; where they daily study and memorize God's Word; and where they are taught to witness these truths to others. How privileged are the children who have such an education, and what opportunities the Holy Spirit has to convict and empower them for their eternal mission!

1. White, *Education,* page 13.
2. Ibid., page 14.
3. Ibid., page 15.
4. Ibid., pages 15, 16.
5. Ibid., page 21.
6. Ibid., page 20.
7. Ibid., page 30.
8. Ibid., page 21.
9. Ibid.
10. Ibid., page 15.
11. White, *My Life Today,* page 250.

Chapter 6
Counterfeit Education

While serving some years ago on a conference committee, Colin had voiced objections to the proposed ordination of a young pastor, for he knew all too well the new-theology leanings of this pastor. A meeting was arranged with the pastor and key conference officials; at which the young pastor deftly sidestepped the issues before the men, who at the time had little insight into the subtleties of the issues then beginning to confront the church.

After the meeting, all left the room but Colin and the young pastor. Colin turned to him and suggested, "They (the conference officials) are unaware of it, but you and I know, that doctrinally, you and I represent two different trains, on two different tracks, headed in two separate directions." With a knowing smile of triumph the pastor agreed, and shortly afterward was ordained to the ministry of the Seventh-day Adventist Church, to lead God's precious flock from the special revelation of the gospel entrusted to them.

Deceptive, subtle, and unclear statements often characterize those who teach and preach error. But the trend is to proclaim error more and more openly, once the initial deception is received. The deceiver often proclaims loudly, and even indignantly, his loyalty to the Seventh-day Adventist Church, to the Bible, and the writings of Ellen White. But such an assertion does not deceive the true students of God's Word, who are frequently accused of making unfair judgments on teachings of those who lull the people into the false security of the Laodicean slumber.

True education, by its very nature, is transparent. It does not deal in double talk. It does not leave the student in two minds as to its meaning. Where doubt is engendered and subtlety is utilized to express thoughts, such bears the unmistakable identity of counterfeit education. It is the use of this type of education that has spearheaded infiltration of the new theology into God's church. Such education is a self-confessed impostor.

The advent of Satan, in the universe, foreshadowed the rise of a counterfeit to every principle of the government of God. When God created Adam and Eve, Satan was ready to test them with his deception and guile. Satan, the father of lies, chose to lead Eve to question the veracity of God's Word. Ironically, Eve first argued on God's side.

> And the woman said unto the serpent, We may eat of the fruit of the trees of the garden: but of the fruit of the tree which is in the midst of the garden, God hath said, Ye shall not eat of it, neither shall ye touch it, lest ye die (Genesis 3:2, 3).

But Satan was far too wily for her; and she had soon accepted the word of Satan, and rejected the word of God.

> It was distrust of God's goodness, disbelief of His word, and rejection of His authority, that made our first parents transgressors, and that brought into the world a knowledge of evil. It was this that opened the door to every species of falsehood and error.

> Man lost all because he chose to listen to the deceiver rather than to Him who is Truth, who alone has understanding.[1]

Thus commenced six thousand years of the choice between the pure Word of God and Satan's admixture of truth and error.[2] We have seen throughout the generations that Satan has succeeded in turning the people of God from the purity of truth.[3]

If he could do this forever, there could never be a generation to reflect God's character, and thus no generation would be ready to receive the seal of the living God. No authentic message could be proclaimed to the farthest bounds of the earth; and no generation would be prepared to live in the time of Jacob's trouble without a Mediator. Thus education— God's perfect program and methods alone—can provide the basis for preparing a people to enter the courts of heaven.

Ever since his success in Eden, Satan has based his assault on man by attacking the veracity of God's Word. For every truth of God Satan has a well-established counterfeit. But in no area has Satan's thrust been more specifically directed than in education, because of its unity with redemption. Satan's false principles of education are calculated to lead man to eternal destruction.

History is replete with evidence that the purity of God's educational program has been eroded, when teachers become enamored with that which is not from the fountain of truth. One of the most emphatic statements ever written by Ellen White is a solemn warning against such erosion.

> Those who seek the education that the world esteems so highly, are gradually led further and further from the principles of truth until they become educated worldlings. At what a price have they gained their education! They have parted with the Holy Spirit of God. They have chosen to accept what the world calls knowledge in the place of the truths which God has committed to men through His ministers and prophets and apostles. And there are some who, having secured this worldly education, think that they can introduce it into our schools. But let me tell you that you must not take what the world calls the higher education and bring it into our schools and sanitariums and churches. We need to understand these things. I speak to you definitely. This must not be done.[4]

Unfortunately, the members of God's church through the ages have often felt an inferiority to the "wise" men of the world; and, urged on by natural curiosity, they have often been drawn to spend much time imbibing the spurious philosophies, while spending less and less time in contact with the Word of God. Such face the danger of accepting error as truth; and, then, with great excitement, they hasten to give their new and intriguing insights to their unprepared students. These concepts are often accepted readily as new light, because the student is unaware that what he is hearing for the first time is really ancient heresy.

Paul foresaw that in the last days there would be in God's church a craving by many to hear error and to have teachers of error.

> For the time will come when they will not endure sound doctrine; but after their own lusts shall they heap to themselves teachers, having itching ears; And they shall turn away their ears from the truth, and shall be turned unto fables (2 Timothy 4:3, 4).

Error is much more palatable than truth to the carnal mind because error, originated by Satan, is not calculated to convict of sin, nor does it challenge to a transformation of life through divine power. Truth, on the other hand, "is quick, and powerful, and sharper than any two-edged sword, piercing even to the dividing asunder of soul and spirit, and of the joints and marrow, and is a discerner of the thoughts and intents of the heart" (Hebrews 4:12).

Because truth demands an awakening to the spiritual impoverishment of carnal security, it cries out for transformation which is abhorrent to many. This aversion leads to hostility to truth and to those who teach and preach it, so that the observation of Isaiah becomes increasingly true in the last days of this world's history.

> Justice is rebuffed and flouted while righteousness stands aloof; truth stumbles in the market place and honesty is kept out of court, so truth is lost to sight, and whoever shuns evil is thought a madman (Isaiah 59:15, NEB).

God's education and the principles of truth are always simple, and therefore have little appeal to the vain heart of man, whose pride is reinforced by the sophisticated hypotheses of men. Thus only the truly convicted educator is willing to lean wholly upon the Source of truth and upon God's Word for his educational direction. Only such a teacher sees God's Word as the true wisdom that his students can safely study. He safeguards his students against that which is not consistent with the revelation of God.

Just as in the days of ancient Judah, those who reject truth and teach and practice error will be held in awful accountability.

> Run ye to and fro through the streets of Jerusalem, and see now, and know, and seek in the broad places thereof, if ye can find a man, if there be any that executeth judgment, that seeketh the truth; and I will pardon it. And though they say, the LORD liveth; surely they swear falsely. O LORD, are not Thine eyes upon the truth? Thou hast stricken them, but they have not grieved; Thou hast consumed them, but they have refused to receive correction: they have made their faces harder than a rock; they have refused to return (Jeremiah 5:1–3).

Wherefore God also gave them up to uncleanness through the lusts of their own hearts, to dishonor their own bodies between themselves: Who changed the truth of God into a lie and worshipped and served the creature more than the Creator, who is blessed forever (Romans 1:24, 25).

There are certain practices that lead into erroneous pathways.

Without the influence of divine grace, education will prove no real advantage; the learner becomes proud, vain, and bigoted.[5]

Human error frequently commences with a nonbiblical view of the nature of man. Education and social services are predominantly built upon the view that either man is born with no moral disposition (e.g., the behaviorism of Skinner), or that he is born innately good (e.g., the nondirective theory of Rogers). But these false views are firmly condemned as erroneous by Inspiration. The behaviorist view is unacceptable in the light of the following:

It is impossible for us, of ourselves, to escape from the pit of sin in which we are sunken. Our hearts are evil, and we cannot change them. "Who can bring a clean thing out of an unclean? not one" (Job 14:4). "The carnal mind is enmity against God: for it is not subject to the law of God, neither indeed can be" (Romans 8:7). Education, culture, the exercise of the will, human effort, all have their proper sphere, but here they are powerless. They may produce an outward correctness of behavior, but they cannot change the heart; they cannot purify the springs of life. There must be a power working from within, a new life from above, before men can be changed from sin to holiness. That power is Christ.[6]

The innate goodness view of man is inconsistent with the following:

The idea that it is necessary only to develop the good that exists in man by nature, is a fatal deception.[7]

Indeed, the Bible concludes that the natural man inescapably moves in pathways that alienate from God; and apart from Christ, he is helpless and hopeless.

I am the vine, ye are the branches: he that abideth in Me, and I in him, the same bringeth forth much fruit: for without Me ye can do nothing (John 15:5).

As it is written, There is none righteous, no, not one (Romans 3:10).

Can the Ethopian change his skin, or the leopard his spots? then may ye also do good, that are accustomed to do evil (Jeremiah 13:23).

Behold, I was shapen in iniquity; and in sin did my mother conceive me (Psalm 51:5).

On the other hand, there are those who believe that because man is naturally helpless he must remain in his state of sinful disobedience. But such a belief is clearly denied by Scripture, which reveals that divine power is available to all who submit their will to Christ, to transform the life and procure victory over sin.

Let not sin therefore reign in your mortal body, that ye should obey it in the lusts thereof. For sin shall not have dominion over you: for ye are not under the law, but under grace (Romans 6:12, 14).

For I am persuaded, that neither death, nor life, nor angels, nor principalities, nor powers, nor things present, nor things to come, nor height, nor depth, nor any other creature, shall be able to separate us from the love of God, which is in Christ Jesus our Lord (Romans 8:38, 39).

There hath no temptation taken you but such as is common to man: but God is faithful, who will not suffer you to be tempted above that ye are able; but will with the temptation also make a way to escape, that ye may be able to bear it (1 Corinthians 10:13).

Not only does a wrong view of the nature of man and God's saving grace affect the educator's approach, but there is always a temptation to validate education by the prevailing climate of society. In so doing, there is a regression away from God's education and toward the education of the world.

The Creator of the heavens and the earth, the Source of all wisdom, is second to none. But supposedly great authors, whose works are used as textbooks for study, are received and glorified, though they have no vital connection with God. By such study man has been led into forbidden paths. Minds have been wearied to death through unnecessary work in trying to obtain that which is to them as the knowledge which Adam and Eve disobeyed God in obtaining.[8]

Teachers who are thus influenced surely fall into this category that's described by Paul:

Now the end of the commandment is charity out of a pure heart, and of a good conscience, and of faith unfeigned: From which some having swerved have turned aside unto vain jangling; Desiring to be teachers of the law; understanding neither what they say, nor whereof they affirm (1 Timothy 1:5–7).

Often in their enthusiasm to be acclaimed by secular educators, many Christian teachers part with the God-centered curriculum of true education, and embellish their offerings with spurious worldly concepts. They then flatter themselves that they are challenging the minds of their students with a more advanced education that will better fit the students to meet the challenges within the world. But the results are eternally fearful. By this education, these inexperienced students are much more likely to imbibe the philosophies of the world rather than be prepared to meet them. It is no wonder that such education is strongly condemned.

Is it the Lord's purpose that false principles, false reasoning, and the sophistries of Satan should be kept before the minds of our youth and children? Shall pagan and infidel sentiments be presented to our students as valuable additions to their store of knowledge? The works of the most intellectual skeptic are the works of a mind prostituted to the service of the enemy; and shall those who claim to be reformers, who seek to lead the children and youth in the right way, in the path cast up for the ransomed of the Lord to walk in, imagine that God would have them present to the youth for their study that which will misrepresent His character and place Him in a false light? Shall the sentiments of unbelievers, the expressions of dissolute men, be advocated as worthy of the student's attention, because they are the productions of men whom the world admires as great thinkers? Shall men professing to believe in God gather from these unsanctified authors their expressions and sentiments, and treasure them up as precious jewels to be stored away among the riches of the mind? God forbid.[9]

One of the tragedies of this approach is exemplified in the experience of a young man, bound for a secular university, who decided to spend one more year at a Christian college to fortify his understanding of truth, by studying deeply in theology classes. Before the year was concluded, he had not only failed to receive the fortification that he so much looked for in his Bible classes, but he had also become skeptical and agnostic in his perspective. Instead of answering the great questions of life, some of the teachers had presented questions of doubt for which he had been supplied no answer. Instead of illuminating the life of this talented youth, his teachers destroyed his faith. What response will these teachers give when called to answer in the final judgement?

Some of the causes of counterfeit education involving Seventh-day Adventist schools are as follows:

1. **Starting with premises that are not founded upon God's Word**

   Men fall into error by starting with false premises and then bringing everything to bear to prove the error true.[10]

2. **Egocentricity and intellectual pride**

   The teachers in our schools are today in danger of following in the same track as did the Jews in Christ's day. Whatever may be their position, however they may pride themselves upon their ability to teach, unless they open the chambers of the soul temple to receive the bright rays of the Sun of Righteousness, they are written in the books of heaven as unbelievers. By precept and example they intercept the rays of light that would come to the students. Their danger is in being self-centered, and too wise to be instructed.[11]

3. **Emphasis upon worldly wisdom, practices, and traditions**

   It is so easy to drift into worldly plans, methods, and customs and have no more thought of the time in which we live, or of the great work to be accomplished, than had the people in Noah's day. There is constant danger that our educators will travel over the same ground as did the Jews, conforming to customs, practices, and traditions which God has not given. With tenacity and firmness, some cling to old habits and a love of various studies which are not essential, as if their salvation depended upon these things. In doing this they turn away from the special work of God and give to the students a deficient, a wrong education.[12]

4. **Failure to make God the central theme of their studies**

    Cold, philosophical speculations and scientific research in which God is not acknowledged are a positive injury. And the evil is aggravated when, as is often the case, books placed in the hands of the young, accepted as authority, and depended upon in their education, are from authors avowedly infidel. . . . The study of such books is like handling black coals; a student cannot be undefiled in mind who thinks along the lines of skepticism.[13]

5. **Emphasis placed upon human wisdom**

    Today young men and women spend years in acquiring an education which is as wood and stubble, to be consumed in the last great conflagration.[14]

6. **Failure of teachers to obtain a thorough knowledge of God's Word**

    Now the end of the commandment is charity out of a pure heart, and of a good conscience, and of faith unfeigned: From which some having swerved have turned aside unto vain jangling; Desiring to be teachers of the law; understanding neither what they say, nor whereof they affirm (1 Timothy 1:5–7)

7. **Emphasis placed upon philosophies and theological studies**

    As a preparation for Christian work many think it essential to acquire an extensive knowledge of historical and theological writings. They suppose that this knowledge will be an aid to them in teaching the gospel. But their laborious study of the opinions of men tends to the enfeebling of their ministry rather than its strengthening.[15]

God's education is simple; Satan's is complicated. God's education brings conviction of sin; Satan's condones sin. God's education gives power to gain victory over sin; Satan's leads to weakness and the continuation of sinful practices. God's education brings peace while Satan's education multiplies perplexities. God's education fits His disciples for their eternal home; Satan's education leads to destruction.

1. White, *Education*, page 25.
2. See chapter entitled, "Foolishness and Wisdom."
3. See chapter entitled, "Education and Reformation."
4. White, *Fundamentals of Christian Education*, pages 535, 536.
5. White, *Counsels to Parents, Teachers, and Students*, page 94.
6. White, *Steps to Christ*, page 18.
7. Ibid., pages 18, 19.
8. White, *Counsels to Parents, Teachers, and Students*, page 444.
9. Ibid., pages 25, 26.
10. White, *Testimonies for the Church*, Volume 7, page 181.
11. White, *Counsels to Parents, Teachers, and Students*, page 372.
12. White, *Testimonies for the Church*, Volume 6, page 150.
13. White, *Counsels to Parents, Teachers, and Students*, pages 423, 424.
14. Ibid., page 444.
15. Ibid., page 379.

SECTION B

Education of the Total Man

Chapter 7
Physical Education

As lads we received the "best" education in the world, or so we thought. It was a highly academically-centered curriculum, allowing us to avoid the practical arts, which we detested and thought were outside the realm of our talents. The lack of education in practical areas of life can be fully attested to by our wives. If it had not been for some home training, especially in gardening, this essential facet of education might have been wholly neglected in our lives.

The influence of the ancient Greek mentality has had an amazing and persisting effect upon educational thought and practice, based upon four erroneous assumptions.

1. The soul (mind) is immortal and good; therefore, activities of intellectual education are liberal and fit for a free man.

2. The body is evil; and, therefore, work is degrading.

3. The slaves are fit only to do the physical work; therefore, sports and activities of war provide the exercise required by the free man.

4. The philosopher is of preeminent value to the needs of the state. The Greeks attempted to build a society, in which the activities of the mind were considered vastly superior to those associated with the musculature of the body. This mentality persisted into the Middle Ages when the serfs were the illiterate workers, while the noblemen were educated intellectually and provided for their physical needs by sports and simulated war games. Indeed, as late as the early part of this century, academic pursuits were given the more elevated term of *education,* and practical pursuits were the lower category of *training.* While this distinction may not be as overt today, it still persists and is especially strong even among many Christians who see the professions as of a higher level of life than

the trades. But sports have never had the negative connotation in secular education that's sometimes ascribed to work, as was evidenced in the ancient Olympic games and in modern sporting contests.[1]

The divine educational pattern has never encompassed competitive sports, for rivalry is inimical to the kingdom of love and righteousness. Yet physical education is fundamental to true God-centered education.[2]

> Physical health lies at the very foundation of all the student's ambitions and his hopes. Hence the pre-eminent importance of gaining a knowledge of those laws by which health is secured and preserved.[3]

> Let none who profess godliness regard with indifference the health of the body, and flatter themselves that intemperance is no sin, and will not affect their spirituality. A close sympathy exists between the physical and the moral nature. The standard of virtue is elevated or degraded by the physical habits.[4]

In the Garden of Eden the pattern for mankind was given. Physical exercise was established upon the principle of useful manual labor. This principle became integral to every God-centered movement throughout history.

> In establishing our schools out of the cities, we shall give the students an opportunity to train the muscles to work as well as the brain to think. Students should be taught how to plant, how to gather the harvest, how to build, how to become acceptable missionary workers in practical lines. By their knowledge of useful industries they will often be enabled to break down prejudice; often they will be able to make themselves so useful that the truth will be recommended by the knowledge they possess.[5]

> Useful manual labor is a part of the gospel plan. The Great Teacher, enshrouded in the pillar of cloud, gave directions to Israel that every youth should be taught some line of useful employment. Therefore it was the custom of the Jews, the wealthy as well as the poorer classes, to teach their sons and daughters some useful trade, so that, should adverse circumstances arise, they would not be dependant upon others, but would be able to provide for their own necessities. They might be instructed in literary lines,

but they must also be trained to some craft. This was deemed an indispensable part of their education.[6]

It was God's purpose to alleviate by toil the evil brought into the world by man's disobedience. By toil the temptations of Satan might be made ineffectual and the tide of evil stayed. And though attended with anxiety, weariness, and pain, labor is still a source of happiness and development, and a safeguard against temptation. Its discipline places a check on self-indulgence, and promotes industry, purity, and firmness. Thus it becomes a part of God's great plan for our recovery from the Fall.[7]

Study in agricultural lines should be the A, B, and C of education given in our schools. This is the very first work that should be entered upon. Our schools should not depend upon imported produce, for grain and vegetables, and the fruits so essential to health. Our youth need an education in felling trees and tilling the soil as well as in literary lines. Different teachers should be appointed to oversee a number of students in their work and should work with them. Thus the teachers themselves will learn to carry responsibilities as burden bearers. Proper students also should in this way be educated to bear responsibilities and to be laborers together with the teachers.[8]

As a relaxation from study, occupations pursued in the open air, and affording exercise for the whole body, are the most beneficial. No line of manual training is of more value than agriculture.[9]

Of course, physical education for the Christian is not limited to work, as it also includes:

1. Exercise in missionary endeavor. Just prior to the turn of the century, Ellen White visited a committee at Avondale College, which was discussing suitable "amusements" for the students. She counseled that students should obtain exercise by walking to the various villages some distance away, there to witness their faith.

While we were living at Cooranbong, where the Avondale school is established, the question of amusements came up for consideration. "What shall we do to provide for the amusement of our students?" the faculty inquired. We talked matters over together, and then I came before the students and said to them:

"We can occupy our minds and our time profitably without trying to devise methods for amusing ourselves. Instead of spending time in playing games that so many students play, strive to do something for the Master.

The very best course for you to pursue is to engage in missionary work for the people of the neighborhood and in the near-by settlements."[10]

2. Walking. Those who live near hilly terrain have the opportunity of quality aerobic exercise by brisk walking through the woods or by the countryside. This is one of the best methods, not only of physical exercise but also of spiritual and emotional development.

There is no exercise that can take the place of walking. By it the circulation of the blood is greatly improved.[11]

A walk, even in winter, would be more beneficial to the health than all the medicine the doctors may prescribe.[12]

3. Nature activities. The invigoration and revitalization of a change of location and relaxation in the open air is of great benefit to all. It is necessary to get away from even important responsibilities on a regular basis. Jesus, Himself, demonstrated this.

And he sent away the multitude, and took ship, and came into the coasts of Magdala (Matthew 15:39).

For children, the natural recreation and education in the out-of-doors are a great antidote to artificial and contrived amusements. These also offer fuller opportunity for family ties to be strengthened. As the child learns the joys of communing with nature, he is drawn close to God.

Let several families living in a city or village unite and leave the occupations which have taxed them physically and mentally, and take an excursion into the country, to the side of a fine lake or to a nice grove, where the scenery of nature is beautiful.[13]

There are two other areas of exercise which, though not entirely discounted, nevertheless, can present serious problems. These are the simple ball games and gymnastics.

I do not condemn the simple exercise of playing ball; but this, even in its simplicity, may be overdone.

I shrink always from the almost sure result which follows in the wake of these amusements. It leads to an outlay of means that should be expended in bringing the light of truth to souls that are perishing out of Christ. The amusements and expenditures of means for self-pleasing, which lead on step by step to self-glorifying, and the educating in these games for pleasure produce a love and passion for such things that is not favorable to the perfection of Christian character.[14]

The games that occupy so much of [the student's] time are diverting the mind from study. They are not helping to prepare the youth for practical, earnest work in life. Their influence does not tend toward refinement, generosity, or real manliness. . . .

Exercise in a gymnasium, however well conducted, cannot supply the place of recreation in the open air, and for this our schools should afford better opportunity.[15]

Clearly unsuitable for Christian recreation are competitive and combatant sports. The rivalry and physical abuse of such sports are totally incompatible with Christian grace and spiritual growth. Such militate against the spirit of Christ, which is experienced in service and selflessness.

The public feeling is that manual labor is degrading, yet men may exert themselves as much as they choose at cricket, baseball, or in pugilistic contests, without being regarded as degraded. Satan is delighted when he sees human beings using their physical and mental powers in that which does not educate, which is not useful, which does not help them to be a blessing to those who need their help. While the youth are becoming expert in games that are of no real value to themselves or to others, Satan is playing the game of life for their souls, taking from them the talents that God has given them, and placing in their stead his own evil attributes.[16]

Some of the most popular amusements, such as football and boxing, have become schools of brutality. They are developing the same characteristics as did the games of ancient Rome. The love of domination, the pride in mere brute force, the reckless disregard of life, are exerting upon the youth a power to demoralize that is appalling.[17]

A view of things was presented before me in which the students were playing games of tennis and cricket. Then I was given instruction regarding the character of these amusements. They were presented to me as a species of idolatry, like the idols of the nations.[18]

Because of the international obsession with competitive sports, it will require much more than incidental or casual effort by the parents to provide profitable recreation which will so fulfill the life of the child that he does not seek the vain and worldly.

By no means are Christians alone in seeing the danger of the normative physical education programs in schools and colleges. Many physical education specialists sense the failure of intense competitive sports programs that are a part of most educational systems. Following are the reasons:

1. Too often sporting achievement becomes a major basis of self-worth on the part of students. As the majority of students fail to achieve notoriety, this failure proves counterproductive to the emotional stability of the students.

2. Sports rarely prepare for lifelong exercise. At the end of school or college, most athletes fall back into, at the best, a spasmodic exercise program and, at the worst, a spectator role.

3. Sports tend to become obsessive; and are frequently counterproductive to academic (and spiritual) programs.

4. Sports frequently lead to lifelong and sometimes life-shortening injuries.

The Christian home and school have the most positive options in physical education of the children and youth, options that are far more fulfilling, productive, and useful than competitive games. God's provisions lead to physical, emotional, social, intellectual, and spiritual consequences, which cannot be paralleled by the sports of pagan origin. In the skills that are learned in work and open-air recreation, and in cooperative teamwork that is not established upon the demise or defeat of another, the child is more positively drawn to God and His mission.

1. Thus when Cecil Rhodes, the founder of Rhodesia (now Zimbabwe), endowed his famous Rhodes Scholarships for the top scholars of the British Empire and the United States to study at Oxford University, he stipulated that the scholarships should be awarded only to those who excel in both academic studies and in the field of sports. But he made no requirements for excellence in practical skills.
2. See chapter entitled, "A Balanced Education."
3. White, *Fundamentals of Christian Education,* page 72.
4. White, *Counsels on Health,* page 67.
5. White, *Counsels to Parents, Teachers, and Students,* pages 309, 310.
6. Ibid., page 307.
7. Ibid., page 274.
8. White, *Testimonies for the Church,* Volume 6, page 179.
9. White, *Education,* page 219.
10. White, *Counsels to Parents, Teachers, and Students,* page 549, 550.
11. White, *Testimonies for the Church,* Volume 3, page 78.
12. Ibid., Volume 2, page 529.
13. White, *Counsels to Parents, Teachers, and Students,* pages 346, 347.
14. White, *The Adventist Home,* page 499.
15. White, *Education,* page 210.
16. White, *Counsels to Parents, Teachers, and Students,* pages 274, 275.
17. White, *Education,* page 210.
18. White, *Counsels to Parents, Teachers, and Students,* page 350.

Chapter 8
Agriculture, the ABC of Education

Millennia after millennia agrarian pursuits dominated the occupational and recreational activities of mankind. Survival was centered upon them; and man's dependence upon, and often struggle with, nature constituted the central issue of life. Cities were to be small and widely dispersed, so that the majority of the world's inhabitants lived in rural and semirural locations. Nature, for the most part, was not seriously disturbed, and the ecological balance was naturally maintained.

Hardly could the early geniuses of the Industrial Revolution have been expected to foresee the tidal wave effect of their rather crude mechanical inventions. Surely, none could have predicted the sociopsychological impact of these exciting discoveries, nor the effect upon life's struggles, physical development, and health.

By the early part of the twentieth century, these changes had begun to have a marked impact upon the distribution of mankind. Large industrially-based cities attracted, like a magnet, the increasing number of ruralists, who were forced by economics and advancing technology to leave the soil that had been their heritage for unnumbered generations. All too often the complex psychological and sociological impact of such rapid changes was either not perceived or could not be adequately handled by government or social agencies. In fact, very few of the latter existed; and, when, after World War II, social agencies proliferated, it was far too late to address a problem that now was totally confounded with the other urban issues.

There is no way that the impact of industrialization upon human experience can be adequately evaluated; but recent successful experiments with agriculture as a therapy for the mentally and physically handicapped are indices of the probable contribution of agriculture to harmonious human growth and development. While one may question Thomas Jefferson's claim that agriculture is the most democratic occupation, it is increasingly difficult to ignore the mounting evidence that the pursuits of the soil are basic to human experience.

God has provided a systematic philosophy of agriculture in education. It is surprising that a pursuit so integral to human history has been largely ignored, or perhaps taken for granted even by God's church. Ellen White has given some of the strongest reasons for agriculture in the curriculum.

> Study in agricultural lines should be the A, B, and C of the education given in our schools. This is the very first work that should be entered upon. Our schools should not depend upon imported produce, for grain and vegetables, and the fruits so essential to health.[1]

She elaborated upon this statement by indicating the value of agricultural pursuits in every major segment of life. She declared that it develops practical wisdom, the ability to plan and execute; it strengthens courage, perseverance, and character, while calling forth the exercise of tact and skills.[2] She further sees agriculture's role in contributing to purity, contentment, and a relationship with God.[3]

Ellen White is far from being an isolated voice in extolling the value of agriculture in the purposeful education of the human race. Hill and Struermann, in *Roots in the Soil,* present as their major concern that the complex superstructure of a technological civilization rests upon the group of workers who handle the soil and deal with nature's resources. They claim:

> Discipline, patience, obedience, responsibility and self-reliance are among the morally worthy traits the farmer's mission engenders in him.[4]

Even more recently, Anne Moffatt suggests four positive results of gardening and landscaping:

a. Builds confidence, purpose, and a sense of accomplishment

b. Builds respect for living things

   c. Offers exercise and tangible rewards for efforts

   d. Offers opportunity for planning, budgeting time, and developing responsibility[5]

Anne Moffatt also points out that health-care personnel have discovered that gardening

   a. Helps release tension

   b. Improves self-esteem and builds ego

   c. Teaches new skills

   d. Offers a channel for self-expression[6]

Karl Menninger, the renowned Kansas psychiatrist, maintains

> As far as mental health is concerned, farmers have it all over city dwellers.[7]

It is reasonable to assume that prior to the industrialization of large segments of the world, little attention was given to the extraordinary role of agriculture in the harmonious development of mankind. After all, it is hard to perceive of anything being extraordinary that is the lot (some no doubt felt, the bane) of almost all members of the human race. Thus it is primarily in recent history that the retreat from the soil has been considered a major factor in the great fractures seen in contemporary society. Whereas small farms, with their attendant close-knit family and social units, once covered the expanse of arable America; except for the Amish and their like, the small farm is gone and huge landholdings dominate. Thus millions have been robbed of the helpful effect and therapeutic value of gardening.

In 1907, addressing the students and faculty of Michigan State University, on the fiftieth anniversary of the founding of the first state-sponsored agricultural college, President Theodore Roosevelt said:

> Our school system has hitherto been well-nigh wholly lacking on the side of industrial training, of the training that fits the men for the shop.... Agricultural colleges and farmers' institutes have done much in instruction and inspiration; they have stood for the nobility of labor and the necessity of keeping the muscle and the brain in training for industry.[8]

Significantly, Roosevelt's statement has become a watchcry to some advocates of the critical role for agriculture in education.

> The best crop is the crop of children, the best products of the farm are the men and women raised thereon.[9]

For example, this is Hill and Struermann's claim:

> The chief product of the farms and of agriculture is persons.[10]

Perhaps the most convincing evidence for agriculture in the educational curriculum, ironically, does not come from regular classroom investigation. Rather, it comes from the increasing evidence of success with the physically handicapped, the mentally retarded, the emotionally disturbed, the hardened criminal, and the sick.

As early as 1768, the renowned Philadelphian physician, Benjamin Rush, maintained that digging in the soil could cure the mentally ill. In the nineteenth century, Dr. Gregory, of northern Scotland, claimed cure for insanity by compelling patients to do farm work.[11] Probably the longest continuous use of horticultural therapy is thought to be the Friends Hospital in Philadelphia, which has used this therapy since its foundation in 1813.[12]

The effectiveness of gardening in the restoration of the ill and the maladaptive seems to be compelling. Major claims include

1. Positive results for stroke and accident victims, as well as sufferers of degenerative diseases.[13]

2. Improvement in mental retardation victims.[14]

3. Some success with bitter and apathetic patients.[15]

4. Improvement in psychiatric patients.[16]

5. Development of self-worth in teenagers.[17]

6. Reduction of fear in child patients facing operations.[18]

7. Aid to senior citizens to realize continued usefulness.[19]

8. Reaching the psychologically dangerous criminal.[20]

With this rapidly increasing evidence, and with the spread of horticultural (hortitherapy), agricultural, and garden therapy, the question which confronts the Christian educator is what role in prevention does agriculture play? Has the obvious fragmentation of Western society been in part a result of the retreat from the soil? The answer is a resounding "yes!" The introduction of agriculture (or gardening) into the curriculum, as a continuing basic core subject, must be urgently addressed.

Dr. Howard Brook of the Institute of Rehabilitation Medicine in New York says,

> Gardening is preventative medicine—the kind you can prescribe for yourself.[21]

But is it more than medicine? The pursuits of the soil offer a broad basis for the development of those human characteristics which are essential for the healthy growth of the individual and the stability of society. While the evidence at hand may not yet be conclusive in the ultimate sense, it is indeed impelling, and thoroughly confirming, of God's counsel. First, there is the abundant sociopsychological evidence of an insecure and fragile society, which is generally far removed from its roots in the soil. In the society, the evidence of the dependency syndrome is increasingly apparent. Then, there is the almost irrefutable proof of the success of soil pursuits in human rehabilitation.

Obviously, out-of-doors gardening offers the widest range of benefits for the participants. These benefits include moderate exercise of the major muscle systems of the body, sunshine, and fresh air (except if undertaken in an urbanized area). Not only are these important to physical health, but also to mental and spiritual health.

> Useful occupation was appointed [Adam and Eve] as a blessing, to strengthen the body, to expand the mind, and to develop the character.[22]

However, where climatic or physical reasons make outdoor gardening impossible, the care of indoor plants or plants in a greenhouse may still have considerable therapeutic and preventive value. Dealing with the therapeutic area, Anne Moffatt says,

> The unique satisfaction derived from getting one's hands into the soil—preparing ground, sowing seeds, observing and nurturing growth, reaping harvests and even pulling weeds seems to frequently set the stage for recovery.[23]

But she further points out that the single largest group to benefit from garden therapy is the home gardeners. She identified three valuable antidotes to stress in home gardening: exercise, relaxation, and esthetic enjoyment.[24]

With such wide-ranging benefits to be derived from agricultural pursuits, a strong case can surely be made for the inclusion of agriculture, or attendant education in the core curricula of every school at all levels of education, kindergarten through college. These are based upon God's counsel and the following considerations (see Table 1, page 67).

1. Physical Benefits. Agriculture, along with many other practical and beneficial pursuits, has much advantage over sports, especially team sports. Physical education experts have increasingly recognized the general failure of team sports to establish lifetime patterns of exercise. Gardening offers a lifetime of such beneficial exercise.

Further, gardening offers exercise independent of the pressure usually associated with competitive sports, so that relaxation rather than tension tends to result. The tendency of competition is to place stress upon winning at the expense of another individual or another team. Gardening is intrinsically free from such negative social consequences.

2. Intellectual Benefits. When the early investigators of intelligence began their work, the emphasis was directed toward defining intelligence as a general, inherent, cognitive capacity. However, more recent theorists and investigators no longer accept such a simplistic definition of intelligence. Most educators see a wide range of inherent and acquired factors. Of greatest importance to this book is the increasing emphasis upon practical skills, as an index of intelligence, alongside the verbal, numerical, and theoretical reasoning skills.

For example, Vernon defines two major factors of intelligence (V:ed, verbal -educational; and K:m, kinestheticmechanical). The continued ability to sustain the practical factors along with the theoretical factors leads to the conclusion that theory and application must stand together in good educational practice. While agriculture is by no means the only worthwhile practical skill, it is surely a skill, which more than most skills accommodates the wide range of intellectual capacity of mankind; and, therefore, it should occupy a primary role in applied education.

3. Emotional Benefits. We have yet failed to fully appreciate the devastating psychological effects of the entertainment syndrome upon modern culture. This failure not only dominates our leisure-time activities, but has invaded education, work, the church, and almost all phases of life.[25]

It is just now that we are beginning to realize the destructive psychological effect of living a life built largely around vicarious experiences. Most children have spent thousands of hours in the make-believe experience of television and other entertainment media, while spending little time in their self-initiated experience. Agriculture activities offer an excellent antidote to such mental health hazards.

The experiences in the real world, the basic cause-and-effect lessons, and the personal fulfillment of agriculture, must help preserve mental health and offer experiences in meeting the real issues of life. These lessons significantly contribute to the establishment of self-worth.

4. Spiritual Benefits. The moral benefits of hard work and worthwhile pursuits have long been recognized. The accomplishment of productive tasks and the rewards of honest labor sustain a platform for growth, which will facilitate the choice of the worthwhile and the valuable. Idleness, indolence, and failure to achieve worthwhile ends not only threaten the emotional health of an individual, but also predispose the individual to antisocial and often criminal behavior. Agriculture, along with other worthwhile practical programs, can facilitate sound moral and spiritual growth.

While it is not within the scope of this chapter to detail the way agriculture might most effectively be integrated into the school curricula, a number of observations may be helpful:

1. Whenever possible, schools should have sufficient land so that every student may have a small garden of his or her own for which to care.

2. It may be advisable to have some opportunity for group agricultural pursuits, where such social intercourse would be deemed advisable.

3. The success of such programs is postulated upon all teachers engaging in and helping the students in their gardens.

4. Where there is much cold weather, greenhouses should be provided for the students' gardening program.

5. City schools have an even greater responsibility than rural schools to inaugurate garden programs. If existing space does not permit this, greenhouse and houseplant culture may be successfully substituted.

6. Gardening courses should offer increasing levels of theoretical understanding, as well as practical experience.

7. Experimentation with soil enrichment and food quality analysis might also be added at upper levels.

Agriculture should stand beside reading, English, writing, mathematics, and spiritual training, as the core of the educational curriculum. True Christian education will offer every opportunity for students to gain an education in the pursuits of the soil.

1. White, *Testimonies for the Church,* Volume 6, page 179.
2. White, *Education,* pages 112, 220.
3. White, *Counsels to Parents, Teachers, and Students,* page 186.
4. Hill, Johnson D.; Struermann, Walter E.; *Roots in the Soil,* (Philosophical Library, New York, ©1964), page 21.
5. Moffatt, Anne, "Therapy in Plants," *Science Digest,* February 1980, pages 62, 65.
6. Ibid., pages 64, 65.
7. Hall, B. H.; Kenworthy, M. E.; "A psychologist's World," *The Selected Papers of Karl Menninger, M.D.,* (Viking Press, New York, ©1959, page 11.
8. Roosevelt, Theodore, "The Man Who Works With His Hands," *Agricultural Thought in the Twentieth Century,* edited by George McGovern, (The Bobbs-Merrill Co., Inc., ©1967), pages 27–32.
9. Ibid., page 32.
10. Hill & Struermann, op. cit., page 22.
11. Gaylin, Jody "Green-Thumb for the Handicapped," *Psychology Today,* April 1976, page 118.
12. Moffatt, op.cit., page 65.
13. Gaylin, op. cit.
14. Ibid.
15. Ibid.
16. Moffatt, op. cit., page 62.
17. Ibid.
18. Horn, Jack, "The Green-Thumb Care for Hospital Fears," *Psychology Today,* page 99.
19. Moffatt, op. cit.
20. Leon, Coralee "Earth, The Healing Power of Gardening," *House and Garden,* February 1976, page 67.
21. Ibid.
22. White, *Education,* page 21.
23. Moffatt, op. cit., pages 62, 63.
24. Ibid., page 65.
25. See chapter entitled, "Emotional Education."

Table 1

Educational Values of Agriculture

Physical	Intellectual	Emotional	Moral
1. Offers effective exercise	1. Develops practical wisdom	1. Builds confidence	1. Develops character
2. Teaches new skills	2. Develops ability to plan	2. Builds purpose for life	2. Encourages development of purity
3. Calls for exercise of skills	3. Calls for skill in execution of plans	3. Develops a sense of accomplishment	3. Leads to peace with God
4. Develops industry	4. Requires budgeting of time	4. Preserves mental health	4. Strengthens courage and purpose
5. Develops nobility of physical labor	5. Encourages self-reliance	5. Aids recovery from mental illness	5. Develops patience
6. Provides excellent prevention	6. Provides aesthetic enjoyment	6. Eases fears	6. Develops responsibility
7. Aids recovery from accident and illness	7. Offers channel for self-expression	7. Helps to release tension	7. Calls for exercise of tact
		8. Aids relaxation	8. Requires self-discipline
		9. Improves self-esteem	9. Develops service motives
			10. Calls for obedience to rule
			11. Builds respect for living things

67

Chapter 9
Emotional Education

One of the most brilliant students ever encountered by Colin during his years in education was a young elementary school lad who had all the potential for a most successful adult life. Years later he had not fulfilled that promise; and, indeed, many considerably less talented students have achieved much more. Of even greater sorrow is the fact that he no longer fellowships with the members of God's church.

It has been the observation of the authors that emotional instability, which proved the downfall of this young man, frequently is a major factor, not only in occupational failure but, more importantly, in spiritual declension. This failure may well occur because every form of functional (i.e., not attributable to an organic cause) mental illness has its root in self-centeredness.[1] Insecurity, low self-worth, depression, and anxiety all have deep spiritual consequences. For many, reason is dethroned by the dominance of emotionality.

It should be observed, however, that emotions have an important and valid role to play in life in general, and in spiritual life in particular. Scripture is replete with exhortations to positive emotions.

JOY

> Restore unto me the joy of Thy salvation; and uphold me with Thy free Spirit (Psalm 51:12).

> Yet I will rejoice in the LORD, I will joy in the God of my salvation (Habakkuk 3:18).

PEACE

These things I have spoken unto you, that in Me ye might have peace. In the world ye shall have tribulation: but be of good cheer; I have overcome the world (John 16:33).

Therefore being justified by faith, we have peace with God through our Lord Jesus Christ (Romans 5:1).

LOVE

Beloved, let us love one another: for love is of God; and every one that loveth is born of God, and knoweth God (1 John 4:7).

Herein is our love made perfect, that we may have boldness in the day of judgment: because as He is, so are we in this world (1 John 4:17).

CONTENTMENT

Not that I speak in respect of want: for I have learned, in whatsoever state I am, therewith to be content (Philippians 4:11).

Let your conversation be without covetousness; and be content with such things as ye have: for He hath said, I will never leave thee, nor forsake thee (Hebrews 13:5).

HAPPINESS

Happy is the man that findeth wisdom, and the man that getteth understanding (Proverbs 3:13).

He that keepeth the law, happy is he (Proverbs 29:18).

There are times, however, when what are usually considered to be the negative emotions have an appropriate and useful place in the life of the Christian.

SORROW

> Now I rejoice, not that ye were made sorry, but that ye sorrowed to repentance: for ye were made sorry after a godly manner, that ye might receive damage by us in nothing (2 Corinthians 7:9).

> For godly sorrow worketh repentance to salvation not to be repented of: but the sorrow of the world worketh death (2 Corinthians 7:10).

ANGER

> Be ye angry, and sin not (Ephesians 4:26).

HATRED

> Ye that love the LORD, hate evil (Psalm 97:10).

> A time to love, and a time to hate (Ecclesiastes 3:8).

JEALOUSY

> For I am jealous over you with godly jealousy: for I have espoused you to one husband, that I may present you as a chaste virgin to Christ (2 Corinthians 11:2).

COVETOUSNESS

> But covet earnestly the best gifts: and yet shew I unto you a more excellent way (1 Corinthians 12:31).

Emotions form a vital part of the personality and the individuality of human beings. Emotions are God-given, and when kept under the domination of a sanctified mind and Christ-controlled will, they enrich the ministry of the individual. However, when reason is subservient to emotional moods, great spiritual loss results, which impedes maturity and productivity.

Like most of life's activities, emotional responses are learned largely by modeling. Violent emotions and dramatic emotional swings in the experience of the parent have a significant impact upon the life of the child. They generally lead to one of two negative consequences. Either the child is cowed and repressed by them, or he himself begins to exhibit the uncontrollable behavior of his parent.

Unquestionably, the calm, consistent, unflappable, quiet, strong parent has a great advantage in providing an emotional environment that will offer the maximum opportunity for the child to develop a balanced and maturing life pattern. Even this example, however, does not ensure a balanced cognitive-affective development. The natural tendency of all children is to respond willfully, and sometimes violently to that which crosses their will. Under no circumstances must this self-seeking behavior be reinforced by surrender to the child's tantrums. To do so is to ensure a painful parent-child relationship which frequently never achieves normality, even in later life. More often than not, all other relationships throughout life are seriously impaired, leading to misery both for the child and for those who are close to him.

On the other hand, severe punishment of willful behavior and tantrums might not lead to the desired consequence. The child may build up either overt or repressed rebellion. For most children, the best parental reaction is nonreinforcement. That is, the parent neither reinforces the poor behavior by positive reinforcement (giving in to the child's demands) nor by negative reinforcement (some form of punishment). This response is not always easy for the parent, as the child frequently tests both the patience and the endurance of the parent. But for those parents who endure the difficulties of the early months, and perhaps years, the results are usually satisfying.

However, it must not be concluded that the parent is to seek to develop a passive and spiritless child. The more active and responsive child will likely be the most productive in adult life. Thus the parent seeks to encourage, by word or action, the child to develop an intelligent relationship to life, which, nevertheless, is expressed in warm and friendly human relationships. The optimistic expression of love and concern does much to enrich the life of the individual, and allow for Christlike witness and fellowship.

Those who pattern their lives after the Divine, do not exhibit coldness or exaggerated concern for others, which is often interpreted as interference in other peoples' lives. There is to be an openness, a friendliness, that will be associated with a dignified and sensitive bearing. On the other hand, cyclothymic exhibitions of behavior, which at one time result in heightened flights of elation and at another time in depths of despair, are far removed from the peaceful, contented life that Christ modeled before humanity. He was neither elated by praise nor discouraged by criticism.

The evidence of increasing emotional instability today may be traced to many factors in contemporary society, not the least of which is the entertainment syndrome. The authors first became aware of this in the early 1960s. The Beatles had landed at Sydney Airport to begin their "triumphal" tour of Australia. As the Beatles appeared at the door of the plane, police and airport officials were almost impotent to stop the hysterical response of teenagers, especially girls. The sirens of ambulances soon attested to the fact that some of these adolescents, overcome by emotion, had collapsed helpless, requiring that they be rushed to hospitals, where they had to spend hours, some even days, in recuperation.

Deep emotional responses pull out all the stops of the sympathetic nervous system, including increased heart beat, breathing rate, inhibition of digestion, sweating, and the secretion of huge amounts of adrenalin into the blood stream. The latter acts like a drug to stimulate the individual. Over the long haul, it acts almost like the mainstreaming of potent narcotic drugs; and, like such drugs, the excitement-inducing situations have to be increasingly exaggerated as time passes, to produce the same level of hyperexcitability.

Western society is established, to a large extent, upon the foundation of entertainment—television, the movies, rock music, sports, or reading material—to an extent unknown in the millennia of the past. The nervous system is placed under constant sensory bombardment, in a way that the human sensorium was never meant to endure. The more exaggerated the hyperexcitability during such entertainment, the greater is the depression that must inevitably follow. Often, to avoid this undesired consequence, the individual continually looks for even more exaggerated entertainment.

Many have not seen the connection between the entertainment syndrome and the appalling media expressions of the age. But it is this phenomenon that has led inevitably to hard rock, punk rock, pornographic literature, and X-rated cable television channels, which certainly has been basic to the development of antisocial group patterns and the drug culture.

The responsible parent will not be ignorant of these desperate, last-day efforts of the enemy of human souls to destroy the inhabitants of this planet. The provisions of a simple, practical life, built around close home ties and family activities of a useful nature, are the greatest heritage that parents can bequeath to their children and youths. Because of the nature of contemporary society, parents will need to plan carefully such an environment for their children. It can be done; and, indeed, it must be achieved, if we are to parent a generation which will fully reflect the image of the Creator in this darkest age.

In 1974, a Newsweek article briefly addressed the massive mental health problems of children and youths. The article pointed out:

> By the most conservative estimate, at least 1.4 million children under the age of 18 have emotional problems of sufficient severity to warrant urgent attention. As many as 10 million more require psychiatric help of some kind if they are ever to achieve the potential that medical progress on other fronts has made possible. "If we used really careful screening devices," says Dr. Joseph D. Noshpitz, president of the American Academy of Child Psychiatry, "we would probably double and maybe treble the official statistics."
>
> The hard core of these children are those who are autistic or schizophrenic. They are helplessly withdrawn from reality, and exist in an inner world that is seldom penetrated by outsiders. More than 1 million other children are hyperkinetic.[2]

The role of passive education was dramatized in the same article.

> In today's push-button society children tend to learn about the world around them vicariously by television. "Many of our children and young people have been everywhere by eye and ear," notes a recent report of the Joint Commission on Mental Health of Children, "and almost nowhere in the realities of their self-initiated experiences." And much of what the children see is the vivid depiction of war, violence and social upheaval; aggression has become one of the most pervasive childhood experiences of all, says Dr. Ebbeson of the University of California at San Diego. "Children learn abnormal behavior from observing other people," the California psychologist contends. "The more

aggression a child is exposed to, the more likely that he himself will be aggressive."[3]

A more recent *Reader's Digest* article offers even more startling evidence of the devastating effect of television upon the minds of children and youths.

> Television ranks behind only sleep and work as a consumer of our time. In fact, according to the 1982 Nielsen Report on Television, the average American family keeps its set on for forty nine and a half hours each week. The typical youngster graduating from high school will have spent almost twice as much time in front of the tube as he has in the classroom—the staggering equivalent of ten years of forty hour weeks. He will have witnessed some 150,000 violent episodes, including an estimated 25,000 deaths.[4]

The article further declared:

> U.S. Surgeon General Jesse L. Steinfeld declared, "The casual relationship between televised violence and antisocial behavior is sufficient to warrant immediate remedial action." Last May the National Institute of Mental Health (NIMH) issued a report summarizing over 2,500 studies done in the last decade on television's influence on behavior. Evidence from the studies—with more than 100,000 subjects in dozens of nations—is so "overwhelming," the NIMH found that there is a consensus in the research community "that violence on television does lead to aggressive behavior."[5]

Is there any place for television in the Christian home? The negative consequences clearly outweigh the positive advantages; for passive education by the media clearly leads to frightening consequences in every facet of human life.

PHYSICAL

Television greatly restricts natural exercise, which adversely affects physical growth and development.

EMOTIONAL
Television predisposes to mental illness because much experience is vicarious rather than in the real world.

SOCIAL
Television greatly inhibits normal social interaction in the home.

INTELLECTUAL
Television encourages passive education rather than quality hands-on education.

SPIRITUAL
Television replaces the time most appropriately set aside for home worship and Christian fellowship.

An environment rich in experiences in the real world is essential for secure emotional growth. Parents and teachers do well to help the child avoid excessive imaginary situations, so as to limit the possibility of emotional breakdown in later life.

1. For a more detailed investigation of this topic, see *Family Crisis—God's Solution,* also by Drs. Standish.
2. Clark and Mott, "Troubled Children: The Quest for Help," *Newsweek,* April 8, 1974, page 52.
3. Ibid., pages 53, 54.
4. Methvin, Eugene H., "T.V. Violence: The Shocking New Evidence," *Readers Digest,* January 1983, page 50.
5. Ibid.

Chapter 10
Social Education

The adult adjustment to human personal relations is often reflected in the early interplay of social forces in childhood. The quiet, introspective child may sometimes receive accolades for good behavior, which, indeed, may mark a brooding, frustrated, and extremely dangerous maladaption. Thus some of the most brutal and repetitive crimes have been committed by quite apparently docile, but terribly driven, individuals. Behind that apparently passive mask is a mind that's twisted and hopelessly deranged by a passion to be noticed and to be famous. The sensational headlines of the media act as a rewarding stimulus to continue ghastly crimes until the criminal is eventually apprehended by law enforcement officers.

The child who turns inward usually does so for one of three reasons. First, he may be managed by overbearing and coercive parents, who, as he grows older, frequently spend considerable effort in detailing both to him and to others his faults, weaknesses, and inadequacies. Such parents often express their fear that the child will amount to nothing, will disgrace the family, and will never make anything of himself. The frequent result is the development of a crushed will, or a repressed personality, of a child who never develops sound self-image or self-worth. This personal depreciation is expressed in poor social relations and increasing social maladaption. Deprived of self-respect in adolescence or young adulthood, he is likely to lash out in bizarre antisocial behavior which, while not always exhibiting itself in violent crime, leads to terrible consequences, such as marital misery and breakup.

The second reason, is that, such maladaption can also be caused by the overindulgent or the overprotective parent. Such parents often isolate the child from reasonable peer-group social experiences, a situation exacerbated in the small families of modern Western society. Such children tend to become very shy and socially immature; and, like the coerced child, they tend toward introspection and increasingly egocentric behavior patterns. This usually increases fear of failure and a desperate fear of social and peer-group rejection that is manifested in an inability to reach out to others because of an all-consuming fear that his friendship gestures will not be accepted. Such an individual would rather withdraw from social activities than risk any threat to his fragile ego. But, if strongly motivated, his behavior may express itself in all kinds of maladaption, from the hermit to the sadist.

Third, the neglected child may also develop into an introspective, self-centered individual. In contemporary society, the neglected child may not always be the child from what is normally considered a deprived environment. He may be from the affluent middle class, and has been the recipient of much in the way of material advantages. But he has missed the close family ties so frequently lacking today. Busy parents, carrying heavy responsibilities, are often the worst offenders. The two-parent working home is particularly vulnerable to this syndrome. Things can never take the place of family love and activities.

Colin had preached a sermon on Christian responsibility. The following Monday he received a terse note from his business manager. "Because of the sermon you preached Sabbath, I'm losing the best secretary we have in the office." Colin was a little more relieved when he unfolded the note further and found written, "She felt that God was calling her to stay home and care for her two-year-old son." This was surprising because the sermon had mentioned nothing concerning parental responsibility. Puzzled, the author called the secretary into his office. After being reminded that the sermon had not focused upon parental responsibility, she replied, "That is true, but what God said to me in that sermon was 'Whatever you know is right, do it.' On Saturday night my husband and I discussed the need for our boy to have his mother in the home, ahead of carpets and labor-saving devices that we once thought were absolutely necessary." What a wise decision! Nothing can take the place of the love, the care, and teaching in the home.

How contrasting was the mother, in Cleveland, Ohio, who, early one morning, arrived at the home of our friends, who had advertised a baby-sitting service. She had brought her 2-week-old baby, so that she could resume her working career. She had not investigated the people who may care for her child. They were complete strangers to her, but apparently their price was acceptable. Such an action represents an irresponsibility that is frequently the basis of dire consequences in the life of the child.

Contrary to the opinion of many, the early socialization of the child is far more dependent upon the relationship with parents than upon peer-group relationships. The more stable the home and the more settled the environment, the greater will be the security that is experienced by the child—a security which will help later relationships to be unaffected by uncertainties.

The home appears still to be the best place for acquiring a healthy attachment. At present, no substitute is known for the family in this respect. Frequent interaction with both parents enables the child to accept separation with the least problem. Nevertheless, most children cannot tolerate separation from their mothers before the age of 5; and, for the insecure, this intolerance may continue until age 8, and for some as late as age 10.

> Even the best day care cannot completely neutralize the negative social, emotional, and cognitive effects of motherchild discontinuity.[1]

The parent has the major responsibility in socialization long before the child reaches the age of formal schooling. This interaction is far more important than learning numbers, the letters of the alphabet, or how to tell time; though, of course, these are important. It is very closely linked with emotional security,[2] for the emotionally stable child is almost always the child who has come a long way in his ability to handle social situations in a mature and acceptable manner. Selfishness and ego-defensiveness are at the root of social maladaption; and, as we have stated earlier, education that teaches the joy of sharing and giving is strongly recommended.

Modern society pays less attention to courtesy and etiquette than it once did. While the artificial should be avoided, politeness, consideration, and courtesy should be very much in the education of God's children. Respect for elders and those in authority is very much a part of growing in the path of true godliness. Such courtesy will bespeak of one who is refined in the principles of Jesus, and who is mindful of the needs of others.

Many feel that social education, of necessity, means the opportunity of the child to mix with a large number of children of a wide spectrum of temperament, personalities, and even characters, but such is a misconceived assumption. God has always been jealous of the association of the children of His people.

> As a rule, men and women who have broad ideas, unselfish purposes, noble aspirations, are those in whom these characteristics were developed by their associations in early years. In all His dealings with Israel, God urged upon them the importance of guarding the associations of their children. All the arrangements of civil, religious, and social life were made with a view to preserving the children from harmful companionship and making them, from their earliest years, familiar with the precepts and principles of the law of God.[3]

Ellen White has clearly summarized the main principles for the socialization of the young child.

> In His wisdom the Lord has decreed that the family shall be the greatest of all educational agencies. It is in the home that the education of the child is to begin. Here is his first school. Here, with his parents as instructors, he is to learn the lessons that are to guide him throughout life—lessons of respect, obedience, reverence, self-control. The educational influences of the home are a decided power for good or for evil.[4]

> Happy are the parents whose lives are a true reflection of the divine, so that the promises and commands of God awaken in the child gratitude and reverence; the parents whose tenderness and justice and long-suffering interpret to the child the love and justice and long-suffering of God; and who, by teaching the child to love and trust and obey them, are teaching him to love and trust and obey his Father in heaven.[5]

> Too much importance cannot be placed upon the early training of children. The lessons learned, the habits formed, during the years of infancy and childhood, have more to do with the forma-

tion of the character and the direction of the life than have all the instruction and training of after years.[6]

It becomes clear, from these counsels, that the role of the parents is the primary role in the social development of the child, far exceeding that of peer-group influences, especially in the earlier years. Even in later years, the parents must still acknowledge the primacy of their role in this critical area of development. As the child grows older, appropriately the child reaches out more and more to those of his own age group. The parents, however, have the most solemn responsibility to monitor the moral character of the child's companions. In an age where peer-group pressures are often the dominant influence upon the youths, earnest efforts to develop wise decision-making resources and strength of character are essential in the earlier childhood years.

God intended that His children be social creatures. The creation of a wife for Adam makes that clear.

> And the LORD God said, It is not good that the man should be alone; I will make him a help meet for him (Genesis 2:18).

It is God's plan that, in the most natural and selfless way, His children will be able to reach out to humanity, to serve and minister to them. God realizes that the joy of giving is the greatest gift that human beings can have. Ease of social relationship, an openness to fellowship with others, a disinterested concern for their well-being and good, a freedom to reach out without the fear of rejection, all are critical characteristics of the ones whom the Lord will use mightily to carry the torch of hope and salvation to a desperately needy world.

God's plan does not envisage social intercourse for vain pleasure, nor for popularity, prosperity, or advantage; but the development of social skills, courtesy, and etiquette, to be used in service for God and man, is essential. Parents go a long way toward laying a foundation upon which the effectiveness of the witnessing of the child will be determined.

1. Moore, Raymond S., et al., *School Can Wait*, (Brigham Young University Press, © 1979), page 27.
2. See the chapter, entitled "Emotional Education."
3. White, *The Ministry of Healing*, page 403.
4. White, *Counsels to Parents, Teachers, and Students*, page 107.
5. White, *The Ministry of Healing*, pages 375, 376.
6. Ibid., page 380.

Chapter 11
Intellectual Education

Some have been inclined to consider a demanding intellectual education as inimical to Christian education. Perhaps this feeling has resulted from the fact that intellectualism has often proved to be the enemy of true Christian faith. Many who have achieved distinguished academic attainments have chosen to lean upon their own understanding, and have drifted away from simple trust in Jesus and unwavering confidence in His Word. In fact, so common is this among those who have achieved academic attainments that it probably would not do an injustice to Matthew 19:24 to vary the words of Jesus as follows:

> It is easier for a camel to go through the eye of a needle, than for a highly educated man to enter the kingdom of God.

Yet ignorance is not godliness! The mind has been given us to develop to the glory of God. Some have seen God's choice as frequently among the less educated classes, e.g., Elijah, Elisha, the disciples. However, God has also used the highly educated men such as Moses, Paul, and Luther. God chooses to use the most committed persons, whatever their education. None were kept in ignorance. One has only to read the writings of men such as Peter and John to discover this fact. Whether the formal education has been little or great, Christianity demands, of its adherents, a strong attention to intelligent growth in the knowledge, nurture, and admonition of the Lord. Our successful ministry for Him is determined by such a commitment.

God requires the training of the mental faculties. He designs that His servants shall possess more intelligence and clearer discernment than the worldling, and He is displeased with those who are too careless or too indolent to become efficient, well-informed workers. The Lord bids us love Him with all the heart, and with all the soul, and with all the strength, and with all the mind. This lays upon us the obligation of developing the intellect to its fullest capacity, that with all the mind we may know and love our Creator.

If placed under the control of His Spirit, the more thoroughly the intellect is cultivated, the more effectively it can be used in the service of God. The uneducated man who is consecrated to God and who longs to bless others can be, and is, used by the Lord in His service. But those who, with the same spirit of consecration, have had the benefit of a thorough education, can do a much more extensive work for Christ. They stand on vantage ground.[1]

It will be noticed that the education that God ordains is not for self-centered exaltation or personal pride, but for the glory of God and witness to humanity. Paul declares:

Let no man deceive himself. If any man among you seemeth to be wise in this world, let him become a fool, that he may be wise. For the wisdom of this world is foolishness with God. For it is written, He taketh the wise in their own craftiness. And again, the Lord knoweth the thoughts of the wise, that they are vain (1 Corinthians 3:18–20).

Thus, while it is a divine imperative that all put their minds to the stretch, this instruction does not envisage an education that samples deeply the errors of secular education, but one which focuses upon the development of knowledge and wisdom, consistent with and centered upon the Word of God.

As we come to the close of human history and as the church faces the challenge of a global work yet to be finished, an educated core of fully committed people is necessary to fulfill the gospel commission, under the mighty power of the Holy Spirit.

The times demand an intelligent, educated ministry, not novices. ... The world is becoming educated to a high standard of literary attainment. ... This state of things calls for the use of every power of the intellect; for it is keen minds, under the control of Satan, that the minister will have to meet.[2]

Those who desire to give themselves to the work of God, should receive an education and training for the work, that they may be prepared to engage in it intelligently.[3]

In our chapter entitled, "Childhood Education," attention is drawn to the importance of educating the child in decision-making. Some years ago an irate mother phoned Colin. Her daughter had been a student at the college of which he was president. Sadly, the daughter had chosen a pathway that led her into unChristian activities, and she eventually withdrew from the college. In the course of the conversation, Colin asked the mother if she had educated her daughter to make wise decisions. After some hesitation, the mother said, "Yes. Not long before she left for college, she told me she wanted to go to a dance. I told her to pray about it, and make her decision. A couple of hours later she came back and said she still wanted to go to the dance. Of course, I didn't permit her to go."

That brief dialogue told the story of a mother who had not educated her daughter in good decision-making; and, thus, in late adolescence the daughter was still under the coercive domination of her mother. It was hardly surprising that when she went to college, without the parental control, this young lady chose the tragic pathway of the world.

Early education in decision-making begins with the infant learning cause-and-effect relationships. As the child becomes mobile, the parent realizes that greater danger looms. The child must learn quickly what these dangers are, if he is to survive. Usually he learns quickly the verbal stimuli that warn of danger.

Later the parent begins to supply reasons for action. "You cannot play with Johnny *because we're about to have supper.*" It may be as simple as that, but the parent should not leave a doubt as to the reason for a parental decision. Even more often overlooked by parents and teachers is the giving of a reason when the answer is "yes." The child almost never asks a reason for a positive response; but, even here, the child needs to understand that the parent has a reason for the decision. If the child has to ask "Why?" it is likely the parent will have to give an unthoughtout answer, or simply say "Because I told you so." Such a response only causes frustration to the child, and does not help him in his understanding of how

Table 1

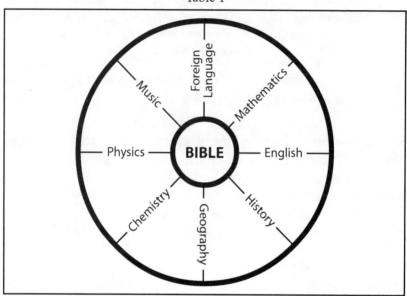

valid decisions are made. Parents err when they give decisions in anger or in haste, for such behavior will tend to be repeated in later life by the child.

As the child matures, he may be given opportunity to make some decisions for himself. In this initial period never should these explorations into decision-making be in moral or spiritual areas. For example, they can be in choice of clothing or in free-time activities. Even here the child will profit from dialogue concerning the reasons for the choice.

There is no magical age at which the child is ready to begin to make significant moral decisions, independent of the parent, but it is essential that this decision-making take place when there are indications of the child's readiness to do so. This time can cause considerable anxiety on the part of the parent, and is, certainly, a time for much prayer. But once the child is given the opportunity to make a decision, he must be allowed to make it, good or bad. Parents must recognize that one poor decision doesn't mean an irreversible failure. Sometimes the parents may have to reverse their thinking a little for future decision-making, but even such a move needs to be done with sensitivity and understanding.

A 14-year-old son of a minister living in a rural area and attending a public school, felt much deprived because of his parents' insistence that he not attend movies. In this pretelevision era, his school friends spent much time discussing the exciting movies they had attended. Eventually this temptation proved too much for this boy. He gathered enough courage to confront his father with the assertion, "Dad, I'm going to go to the pictures (movies)." He waited for the parental veto, but a wise father, who, with his wife, had put much into the fabric of the life of their son replied, "Well, son, for all these years your mother and I have sought to show you God's way, but the time comes when you have to make decisions for yourself." The boy did not attend the movies, an indication of the quality of education that had gone into his earlier education. Such an approach can never succeed without wise childhood education.

These principles must also be translated into the school program. Surely the most critical goal of intellectual education is the development of the child's ability to make intelligent and wise decisions. In the final analysis, this goal overshadows the content that is used to achieve it.

While intellectual education focuses upon the development of a God-centered value system, there must also be an emphasis upon other areas of reasoning and determination of truth. Thus the quality of education must be emphasized within the parameters of a Bible-based curriculum. The Bible must be the hub of education. When the Bible is the basis of education, a vastly superior education results.

> We are rapidly nearing the final crisis in this world's history, and it is important that we understand that the educational advantages offered by our schools are to be different from those offered by the schools of the world.[4]

> God would not have us in any sense behind in educational work. Our colleges should be far in advance in the highest kind of education.[5]

Unless Christ and His principles pervade the curriculum, we do not have Christian education. A talented student teacher had just completed a lesson on the exploits of the English buccaneers, Hawkins and Drake. She had greatly dramatized the success of these men and their crews against the Spanish bullion ships. Being a young lady of good insight, she indicated, in the post-lesson review, that she believed the lesson had been successful. It was pointed out, however, that there was a great weakness which she had failed to perceive. She was asked how many boys in the class she wished to emulate the deeds of Drake and Hawkins. The answer was obvious. "But," she protested, "you can't change the facts of history." It was pointed out that a Christian approach does not change facts, but it does proceed from an entirely different emphasis. "Would she teach the lesson the same way to Spanish children?" The Christian teacher commences with a different perspective. He does not allow his national loyalty to becloud his understanding that God's unlimited love is the same for His creatures of all races. It was explained to this student teacher that she could have emphasized the parents who would never see their sons again, or the wives who would never see their husbands again, or the children who would never see their fathers again. Rather than war being glamorized, it could have been depicted for what it is.

> Satan delights in war, for it excites the worst passions of the soul and then sweeps into eternity its victims steeped in vice and blood. It is his object to incite the nations to war against one another, for he can thus divert the minds of the people from the work of preparation to stand in the day of God.[6]

This is but an example. Every discipline lends itself to a Christ-centered emphasis. Colin was surprised when one of his nursing students indicated that her mathematics teacher had been her most influential spiritual teacher at the college. She had learned more Bible from him than from her theology teachers. Some might question how a mathematics teacher could be both a "Bible" teacher and a mathematics teacher. Colin also was intrigued, and invited the teacher to explain his approach before the faculty. This department chairman left no doubt in his intriguing presentation, as to why he was considered so highly as both a mathematics teacher and a Bible teacher.

All teachers have a divine obligation to learn how to teach their discipline from a God-centered base, before accepting their sacred responsibility. Christian education requires teachers who are fully committed to Christ, who understand the truths of God, who know their academic field from the perspective of divine revelation, and who integrate faith and learning in their classrooom. Only in such an environment can the classroom teacher support the work of the parent in developing the moral basis of Christian decision-making.

1. White, *Christ's Object Lessons,* page 333.
2. White, *Testimonies for the Church,* Volume 5, page 528.
3. White, *Gospel Workers,* page 282.
4. White, *Counsels to Parents, Teachers, and Students,* page 56.
5. Ibid., page 45.

Chapter 12
Spiritual Education

While spiritual education is treated after other forms of education, it, indeed, takes the preeminent place in the education of the child. The spiritual atmosphere in the home, during prenatal development and infancy,[1] largely determines the destiny of the child in the future. If desired consequences do not result in this realm of life, there is no doubt that other areas will also suffer.

In the earlier experience of the Seventh-day Adventist Church, the high ideals and standards maintained led the unconverted and the indifferent to sever their connection with the church. Such a course is by no means automatic today. Thousands of Adventists continue their tenuous connection with the church, when they neither know nor believe its doctrines, and when they live a lifestyle that is inimical to Christian commitment. This lack of commitment has resulted from a number of causes, including the following:

1. The size of many churches makes it easy to live a double life.

2. The church has become a desirable social institution (which, in the right setting, it should be) that allows ready social intercourse with friends and associates.

3. Church members are seldom challenged with the solemnity of church membership and its concomitant responsibilities. Many sermons allow for comfortable sinners.

4. The church's publications, especially for youth, rarely instruct them in true godliness or in the great central truths of our message.

5. The world has dramatically invaded the thinking and lifestyle of many "respected" and leading members of the church.

6. An attitude of indulgence, masquerading as love, exists in most churches.

7. Many churches have allowed, and, indeed, in some cases encouraged, worldly entertainment to come into the churches' activities.

8. Frequently emphasis has been placed upon keeping young people in the church rather than leading them to the footstool of Jesus.

9. Parents, in schools, academies, and churches, plead for indulgence of their children (often not for others), which places heavy pressures on school and church leaders.

10. Church discipline is seldom administered according to true Christian principles.

11. Sin, especially immorality, is no longer seen for the evil that it is.

12. Calls to repentance and reformation are frequently ignored, or even met with hostility.

13. Apostate groups have preached a sin-and-live "gospel," which has been widely accepted.

14. Many teachers and preachers who are influential upon our children and youth (and frequently older members also) have lulled huge numbers of members into Laodicean slumber.

Another creeping spiritual cancer is resulting from the presence of rationalistic humanism in the thinking of many pseudointellectuals in the church. More and more human reasoning and "profound" insights are used to becloud the simple, direct spiritual truths of Scripture. Because of its appeal to intellectual pride, this approach is appealing to many, but it ultimately results in reasoning away even the simplest of truths. The simplicity of Christ and His teachings is the model for all Bible students. It was His knowledge of the Word that magnified His ministry, and led the people to exclaim,

He taught them as one having authority (Matthew 7:29).

Thus Ellen White has counseled:

> In all the sermons and in all the Bible studies, let the people see that on every point a plain "Thus saith the Lord" is given for the faith and doctrines which we advocate.[2]

There are those who believe that God has given man reason to evaluate the Word. Such argue that it is too simplistic to take a surface view of the Word, for we need to discover the deeper meanings of Scripture. The danger of this approach is that there's a major element of truth in it. The Lord wants His children to search the Scriptures diligently.

> My son, if thou wilt receive My words, and hide My commandments with thee; so that thou incline thine ear unto wisdom, and apply thine heart to understanding; yea, if thou criest after knowledge, and liftest up thy voice for understanding; if thou seekest her as silver, and searchest for her as for hid treasures; then shalt thou understand the fear of the LORD, and find the knowledge of God (Proverbs 2:1–5).

However, finite human reasoning can never be used safely to rationalize away a plain "Thus saith the Lord." The counsel must be accepted just as it reads. Sanctified reason can never interpret Scripture. Rather, it takes over at the point where there is no clear testimony from the Lord. At this point, principles are applied to make the best decision possible.

For example, Colin has been involved a number of times in the proposed location, or relocation, of colleges. The "Thus saith the Lord" is clear. These colleges are best located in a rural area, but within range of cities that might be worked from the college outpost. However, the decision of where to actually locate requires sanctified judgment.

It is only reasonable that simplicity marks the basis of true Scriptural understanding. If this were not so, salvation would be for the wise and highly educated. It has been the intriguing observation of the authors that some of the clearest understanding of God's Word has come from those who have had limited formal education; and some of the most confused thinking has come from some of the best educated, even in the field of theology, no doubt because the former have had the simplicity to take the Word as it reads, while many educated men and women lean upon their own wisdom, ignoring the inspired words of Solomon.

Trust in the LORD with all thine heart; and lean not unto thine own understanding. In all thy ways acknowledge Him, and He shall direct thy paths. Be not wise in thine own eyes: fear the LORD, and depart from evil (Proverbs 3:5–7).

The counsel of the Lord in this matter is very plain.

The Bible with its precious gems of truth was not written for the scholar alone. On the contrary, it was designed for the common people; and the interpretation given by the common people, when aided by the Holy Spirit, accords best with the truth as it is in Jesus. The great truths necessary for salvation are made clear as the noonday, and none will mistake and lose their way except those who follow their own judgment instead of the plainly revealed will of God.[3]

Not only is Christian education to center upon the simplicity of the Word, it is also to challenge and inspire the youth to give their lives in totally committed service to God, fulfilling the plea of Paul,

I beseech you therefore, brethren, by the mercies of God, that ye present your bodies a living sacrifice, holy, acceptable unto God, which is your reasonable service. And be not conformed to this world: but be ye transformed by the renewing of your mind, that ye may prove what is that good, and acceptable, and perfect, will of God (Romans 12:1–2).

As parents and educators, we are to envisage the highest possibilities for our children, and, even then, this ideal will fall far short of God's plans for them.

Higher than the highest human thought can reach is God's ideal for His children. Godliness—godlikeness—is the goal to be reached. Before the student there is opened a path of continual progress. He has an object to achieve, a standard to attain, that includes everything good, and pure, and noble. He will advance as fast and as far as possible in every branch of true knowledge. But his efforts will be directed to objects as much higher than mere selfish and temporal interests as the heavens are higher than the earth.[4]

The renowned Humanist educator, Sir Richard Livingstone, once said,

The purpose of education is to equip young people with skill and knowledge for the production of goods, clothing and shelter which go to make up our standard of living. . . . We cannot now be happy without abundance of luxuries, and our educational program should be directed towards enabling all to achieve these.

This is the philosophy so readily discernible in this modern world. This is the logical outcome of Darwinian evolution; it is the child of Marx's Dialectic Materialism; it is the hope of Communism for tomorrow, and the reality of some segments of Western society today.

How different is the concept of education as penned to man, under divine inspiration! Contrast the selfish, ego-centered approach above with the outgoing philosophy of the Christian:

[True education] prepares the student for the *joy of service* in this world and for the *higher joy of wider service* in the world to come.[5]

Or contrast the earthbound attitude of the former with that of the Christian's heaven-centered philosophy:

True education is the inculcation of those ideas that will impress the mind and heart with the knowledge of God the Creator and Jesus Christ the Redeemer.[6]

The pathway of the Christian and that of the worldling are irreconcilable. As Christians, we perceive a different purpose, We experience a different motivation. We look for a different aim. Thus it is that the best of secular education must fall far short of that designed by God for His people. With fearful consequences, the people of God are losing the vision of a soon-coming and redeeming Saviour. We are rapidly showing the inertia depicted by the words, "My Lord delayeth His coming" (Matthew 24:48).

The enthusiasm, the expectancy, the energy, the elevation are lacking. Materialism is gaining a strong hold upon our believers, which, in turn, is being reflected in the outlook of our youth. No longer do we find the majority of Adventist parents working purposefully towards the salvation of their children, and for the preparation of these young ones for Christian service. On the contrary, success is too often adjudged in terms of worldly success—academic, financial, vocational, influential. However much success in these areas might be cause for rejoicing; it can never be the prime object, or the standard, of the truly converted Christian.

The Renaissance saw Western Europe revolt against the concept that this present life is almost meaningless to the Christian. The Humanists of that age rightly pressed the view that man had a very definite purpose in his life on this earth. Mankind today has so taken hold of this concept that now there is almost a complete disregard of the eternal destiny of man. God forbid that His people be swept into this Satan-inspired thinking. We need to give far more than lip service to the task at hand. We must strain every sinew; we must flex every fiber to fulfill the purpose of God.

The present generation of children and youths represents the most crucial generation in the history of God's church. Never has more been expected of a generation; yet, never have there been more unfavorable conditions prevailing. Should this generation fail, the message of the hour would be doomed. Yet, we must confidently look to these young people to take up the challenge, for the Scriptures and the Spirit of Prophecy bear adequate testimony to the successful completion of the gospel proclamation.

Parents, church leaders, church members, and young people must unite to meet the challenge of the times. Only as all throw their energies into the work will the task be completed.

Our Christ-ordained church school and college system was designed to train to this end. There is no other place where such preparation can be received. Then, it is incumbent upon each of us to translate the vision into the reality, where each child is prepared for God's work as he is daily given a vision of Christ his Saviour, and the glory of Christ's salvation.

To achieve these purposes the Christian home and school will

1. **Build character in the students.**

    Character building is the most important work ever entrusted to human beings; and never before was its diligent study so important as now. Never was any previous generation called to meet issues so momentous; never before were young men and young women confronted by perils so great as confront them today.[7]

2. **Be an example to the world.**

    The most important work of our educational institutions at this time is to set before the world an example that will honor God.

94

Holy angels are to supervise the work through human agencies, and every department is to bear the mark of divine excellence.[8]

3. **Lift the standard of truth in the community.**

When properly conducted, church schools will be the means of lifting the standard of truth in the places where they are established; for children who are receiving a Christian education will be witnesses for Christ.[9]

4. **Draw men to Christ.**

There should be men and women who are qualified to work in the churches and to train our young people for special lines of work, that souls may be brought to see Jesus. The schools established by us should have in view this object, and not be after the order of the denominational schools established by other churches, or after the order of worldly seminaries and colleges. They are to be of an altogether higher order, where no phase of infidelity shall be originated, or countenanced. The students are to be educated in practical Christianity, and the Bible must be regarded as the highest, the most important textbook.[10]

1. See chapters entitled, "Prenatal Education" and "The Education of the Infant."
2. White, *Testimonies for the Church*, Volume 6, page 69.
3. Ibid., Volume 5, page 331.
4. White, *Education*, pages 18, 19.
5. Ibid., page 13, italics supplied.
6. White, *Fundamentals of Christian Education*, page 543.
7. White, *Education*, page 225.
8. White, *Counsels to Parents, Teachers, and Students*, page 57.
9. Ibid., page 176.
10. White, *Fundamentals of Christian Education*, page 231.

SECTION C

Developmental Education

Chapter 13
Prenatal Education

Christian parenthood is not accidental. It is planned. This preparation involves economics and living conditions; but, above all, it encompasses the spiritual life of the would-be-parents. Only when the parents are in spiritual unity and harmony with Christ will the Holy Spirit empower them and overshadow the unborn. No better example of this is given in the Scriptures than in the lives of Zacharias and Elisabeth, the parents of John the Baptist.

> Elisabeth was filled with the Holy Ghost (Luke 1:41).

> And his father Zacharias was filled with the Holy Ghost (Luke 1:67).

No doubt, because of this infilling Gabriel could prophesy,

> He shall be great in the sight of the Lord, and shall drink neither wine nor strong drink; and he shall be filled with the Holy Ghost, even from his mother's womb (Luke 1:15).

John the Baptist was a type of Elijah, and gave a message parallel to that which will foreshadow the return of Christ.

> Behold, I will send you Elijah the prophet before the coming of the great and dreadful day of the LORD: And he shall turn the heart of the fathers to the children, and the heart of the children to their fathers, lest I come and smite the earth with a curse (Malachi 4:5, 6).

> And His disciples asked Him, saying, Why then say the scribes that Elias must first come? And Jesus answered and said unto them, Elias truly shall first come, and restore all things. But I say unto you, that Elias is come already, and they knew him not, but have done unto him whatsoever they listed. Likewise shall also the Son of man suffer of them. Then the disciples understood that He spake unto them of John the Baptist (Matthew 17:10–13).

Thus there is great significance in the preparation of husbands and wives who will parent a special generation to take the message of Jesus to the world. There is assurance that, when the Holy Spirit is manifest in the lives of the parents-to-be, this influence will also pervade the life of the prenate, and will greatly maximize the claims of Christ upon the life, protecting the child from a thousand evils.

Sacred questions must be resolved by husband and wife before a child is conceived. Unless they have forged a deep abiding relationship with each other by their individual relationship with Jesus, they are yet unready to begin the parenting of a child. It is irresponsibility to parent a child with the hope of rescuing a shaky and insecure marriage. There is nothing a little, inexperienced infant can do to secure the marriage; and, most likely, he will become the victim of the insecurity of the parents. This situation will, in all likelihood, lead to erratic management of the child and to inconsistency in the expression of both love and discipline. Such behavior sets the stage for serious emotional and social problems in the child's later life.

The importance of the wife's lifestyle during pregnancy is made clear in Scripture. The angel counseled Manoah's wife:

> She may not eat of any thing that cometh of the vine, neither let her drink wine or strong drink, nor eat any unclean thing: all that I commanded her let her observe (Judges 13:14).

The diet and activities of the expectant mother are of paramount impact upon the healthy development of the embryo and the fetus. Just as righteous parents may provide a wonderful benefit for the babe; conversely, parents can be responsible for making it almost impossible for the Holy Spirit ever to gain access to the life of a child.

The parent has about eighteen months to provide bases for a secure and balanced personality and temperament; and, by far, the most important of these are the nine months before birth. The love and security developed in the prenatal environment include the calm and happy disposition of the mother, the healthful and carefully balanced diet she chooses, the avoidance of the use of drugs, spices, or other condiments, the loving relationship with her husband, her secure trust and faith in God, and the daily taking of regular and moderate exercise. Thus mothers are counseled:

> Every woman about to become a mother, whatever may be her surroundings, should encourage constantly a happy, cheerful, contented disposition, knowing that for all her efforts in this direction she will be repaid tenfold in the physical, as well as in the moral, character of her offspring. Nor is this all. By habit she can accustom herself to cheerful thinking, and thus encourage a happy state of mind and cast a cheerful reflection of her own happiness of spirit upon her family and those with whom she associates.[1]

The achievement of such a prenatal environment is the responsibility of the husband just as much as of the wife. His disposition, helpfulness, and loyalty are essential to the new life that is being initiated into their family. Colin recalls a situation when an expectant mother came to counsel with him, shortly after she discovered that her husband was having an affair with another woman. It was almost pointless to urge this devastated spouse to be calm and joyous. As with postnatal responsibilities, the responsibilities of the husband and wife are shared during the prenatal development of their child. Godly partners will second the work of each other in these precious months.

In the complexity of modern living, it is most difficult for choices to be made, to provide the most ideal circumstances for the development of the prenate. During this time, the responsibilities of the wife should be reduced, in order to avoid overexertion and the tension of heavy responsibilities.

The common practice of expectant mothers working up to, or as near to, the time of delivery as possible should be carefully evaluated. The responsibilities and interrelationships at work and home are likely to foster tension, especially during periods when the expectant mother is suffering some physical effects of her pregnancy. Where at all possible, it is wise that a wife greatly reduce, or preferably cease, formal business, industrial, or factory work. This counsel does not foreshadow the mother becoming indolent during these months. On the contrary, activity is profitable; but, as far as possible, it should be activity without the strain or tension that employment outside the home tends to precipitate.

The temperament of the child is greatly affected by that of the mother.

> The thoughts and feelings of the mother will have a powerful influence upon the legacy she gives her child. If she allows her mind to dwell upon her own feelings, if she indulges in selfishness, if she is peevish and exacting, the disposition of her child will testify to the fact. Thus many have received as a birthright almost unconquerable tendencies to evil.[2]

While the placenta is a fine filter, it obviously is not perfect; otherwise no nutrients would be supplied to the rapidly growing fetus. Thus, the emotionality of the mother is quickly transferred to the fetus. When the mother is in a frequent state of hyperexcitement, she automatically secretes adrenalin and other physiologically active substances into her blood system. In turn the blood which is impregnated with the substances reaches the system of the prenate, automatically increasing his hyperactivity. If these incidents occur frequently in the prenate's experience, the foundation of hyperkinetic behavior in later life is securely laid. It is common for parents to relate hyperkinetic behavior to genetic factors; and, while this relationship is possible, it is also likely that it may be traced to the prenatal environment.

It is most unlikely that Christian mothers need counseling concerning the deleterious effect of alcohol, tobacco, and mind-expanding drugs upon the prenate; although, in the United States alone, hundreds of newborn babies die annually from drugwithdrawal symptoms, and tens of thousands of others are permanently injured because of the drug habits of their mothers. However, even Christian mothers need to be most careful in their use of any drugs, including normally prescribed drugs as well as nonprescription drugs, such as headache preparations. The influence of all these should be weighed in the light of their possible effect upon the unborn child.

Of the utmost importance is the sensory input of the mother during pregnancy. This input especially includes what she sees and hears. The mind must be daily reinforced by the sweet messages of the love of Jesus.

At least one or two hours a day contemplating the matchless themes of the Scriptures will prove a great strengthener of faith and contentment. The choice of trust-developing music will also enhance the ideal environment for the expectant mother. This is not the time to spend long periods in the fantasy world of the television, the novel, or other unrealistic media. The wholesomeness of the mind is an essential preparation for parenthood.

Perhaps one other parameter should be explored. The most ideal environment for the child, when he is born, is a rural environment, where there is opportunity for him to readily learn of the God of nature, and where, especially in his early years, he may learn the natural lessons of the garden, while exercising and strengthening his body in the fresh air and sunshine, so abundantly provided. Such environment would also provide the same benefits for the expectant mother and her spouse. The country provides a place for health-enduring exercise in which, depending upon her strength and capacities, she can facilitate as "natural" a birth as possible.

Tremendous issues are at stake in the education of the new generation. It starts with this all-important development before birth. Thus the Lord has provided the clearest counsel for those who are preparing for parenthood. The prenatal education will set the rudder for the child's future character, stability, and success. To initiate a new life into the world without careful personal planning and preparation by parents is a sin.

> [Parents] should understand the principles that underlie the care and training of children. They should be capable of rearing them in physical, mental, and moral health. Parents should study the laws of nature. They should become acquainted with the organism of the human body. They need to understand the functions of the various organs, and their relation and dependence. They should study the relation of the mental to the physical powers, and the conditions required for the healthy action of each. To assume the responsibilities of parenthood without such preparation is a sin.[3]

Upon fathers as well as mothers rests a responsibility for the child's earlier as well as its later training, and for both parents the demand for careful and thorough preparation is most urgent. Before taking upon themselves the possibilities of fatherhood and motherhood, men and women should become acquainted with the laws of physical development—with physiology and hygiene, with the bearing of prenatal influences, with the laws of heredity, sanitation, dress, exercise, and the treatment of disease; they should also understand the laws of mental development and moral training.[4]

If either parent is not willing to take upon himself, or herself, these sober responsibilities, no new life should be brought into the world.

The final generation of parents will have an all-consuming passion—the representation of God's love by practical Christianity, so that their children may choose from the perspective of God's authentic truth. More than anything else, the world needs the restoration of the true Christian home.

1. White, *Mind, Character, and Personality,* page 131.
2. Ibid., page 132.
3. White, *Ministry of Healing,* page 380.
4. White, *Education,* page 276.

Chapter 14
The Education of the Infant

We once had a friend and his wife who were happily expecting the birth of their first child. The husband was adamant. His child was not to be "brain washed" with religion in his early life. When he or she was "old" enough, he would place Christian principles before the child, and let him or her make the decision. No amount of counsel, that Satan does not wait to attack our infants and children, could deter him from his perilous course. The little boy born to them soon exhibited the traits of character that were unmistakably the heritage of Satan. Long before he had reached the age of 10, he was totally beyond the control of his parents. Especially is the deceptive fury of Satan directed at the young of this age. Peter described this situation in the most vivid language:

> Be sober, be vigilant; because your adversary the devil, as a roaring lion, walketh about, seeking whom he may devour (1 Peter 5:8).

It is important to note that this counsel was given to the young of the church. After directing the counsel of the first four verses of the chapter to the senior members of the church, Peter then addressed the youths:

> Likewise, ye younger, submit yourselves unto the elder. Yea, all of you be subject one to another, and be clothed with humility: for God resisteth the proud, and giveth grace to the humble (1 Peter 5:5).

Peter's choice of imagery is not by chance. A pride of lions, seeking a kill, well-knows that large herbivorous animals are a difficult challenge.

Thus, a pride of lions coming upon a herd of Zebra stampedes the herd, for a strong stallion is a formidable match for even these beasts of prey. Very quickly the young and the weak drop back, and soon one is singled out and becomes the hapless victim of the pride. This drama poignantly describes what is happening to our children today. With the fury of one who knows the end is near, Satan ruthlessly attacks the child, from its very beginning. He does not wait for the child to mature, but immediately seeks to reinforce those inclinations to sin, with which every member of the human race is born. So often those who are entrusted with the care of the infant are anesthetized to the early work of Satan.

There are many guidelines that God has given to develop secure, happy children, by whom the claims of Christ will be readily received. These guidelines of necessity begin with the home environment provided by the parents.

> It is by the youth and children of today that the future of society is to be determined, and what these youth and children shall be depends upon the home. To the lack of right home training may be traced the larger share of the disease and misery and crime that curse humanity. If the home life were pure and true, if the children who went forth from its care were prepared to meet life's responsibilities and dangers, what a change would be seen in the world![1]

> The restoration and uplifting of humanity begins in the home. The work of parents underlies every other. Society is composed of families, and is what the heads of families make it. Out of the heart are "the issues of life" (Proverbs 4:23); and the heart of the community, of the church, and of the nation is the household. The well-being of society, the success of the church, the prosperity of the nation, depend upon home influences.[2]

> In His wisdom the Lord has decreed that the family shall be the greatest of all educational agencies. It is in the home that the education of the child is to begin. Here is his first school. Here, with his parents as instructors, he is to learn the lessons that are to guide him throughout life—lessons of respect, obedience, reverence, self-control. The educational influences of the home are a decided power for good or for evil.[3]

> Happy are the parents whose lives are a true reflection of the divine, so that the promises and commands of God awaken in the child gratitude and reverence; the parents whose tenderness and justice and long-suffering interpret to the child the love and justice and long-suffering of God; and who, by teaching the child to love and trust and obey them, are teaching him to love and trust and obey his Father in heaven.[4]

In early life, the infant has no concept of God, other than that which develops from his growing relation with his parents. The love and secure discipline of a Christian home provides an authentic presentation of the character of God, which will, in later life, make him far more receptive to the claims of Christ than if the home is unloving and undisciplined.

The clearest understanding of love comes not so much from the expression of love to him, important though this be, but from the expression of love he perceives between his parents and older members of his family. This is the modeling that he is most likely to follow.

The wise Christian parent will not in any way see himself in competition with his spouse for the affection of the child. It is not uncommon for the infant early to show a slight preference for one spouse or the other, but this preference must not be interpreted as rejection by the other spouse. Almost inevitably, a feeling of rejection by the parent leads to an inappropriate and unproductive relationship. Either that spouse tends to overindulge the child in an attempt to bribe him; or that spouse rejects him, because of his own hurt feelings. How tragic are the results of either response! Under all circumstances, the husband and wife must second each other's efforts, and rejoice in the response of the child to the other. Under no circumstances is it appropriate to force the child into a choice between father and mother. Even in jest, the child should not be asked if he likes Daddy more than Mommy, or the reverse. Infants soon sense rivalry between parents, and use it to their own detriment.

Perhaps the principle of consistency is of the utmost importance to the secure development of the child. This principle includes consistency by each parent in the management of the infant, and consistency by both parents in the child's education. While both facets of training present many challenges; the latter is often the most difficult, for each parent tends to reflect his or her own upbringing; and often one has had a less structured environment than the other. But it is of utmost importance that both parents work together, for the security and salvation of the child is at stake. Each parent must second the efforts of the other, and attempt to resolve any difference of approach in private.

In an age where much controversy exists concerning discipline, God has not left His people in doubt. No infant can be given a sound start in life if he does not quickly begin to realize the parameters of successful living. Thus parents are counseled:

> Before the child is old enough to reason, he must be taught to obey. By gentle, persistent effort, the habit should be established. Thus to a great degree may be prevented those later conflicts between will and authority that do so much to arouse in the minds of the youth alienation and bitterness toward parents and teachers, and too often resistance of all authority, human and divine.[5]

Yet, this does not foreshadow coercive education of the infant, nor an unreasoned approach. For the same author says:

> The object of discipline is the training of the child for self-government. He should be taught self-reliance and self-control. Therefore as soon as he is capable of understanding, his reason should be enlisted on the side of obedience. Let all dealing with him be such as to show obedience to be just and reasonable. Help him to see that all things are under law, and that disobedience leads, in the end, to disaster and suffering.[6]

Yet, God knows that discipline is necessary before the child's reason can be employed; so that early habits of evil, which are so difficult to break, are not formed. There is no valid place for permissiveness in Christian education. Those so educated are like ships without rudders. Having never been adequately disciplined, or guided, in the making of wise decisions, they fail to know how to make choices and decisions of their own, and become tragically insecure, often following the leadership of other unwise youth into activities which weaken the already fragile self-image. The epidemic of insecurity in Western society today can surely be traced in a great extent to the permissiveness of the home, school, and society.

But lest it be felt that the coercive environment is less damaging to the child, it should be pointed out that the child who has the continual imposition of the parental will upon him, so that his own will is crushed, likewise faces a most insecure adolescence and adulthood. Like the child from the permissive home, he has developed few resources to make wise decisions for himself.[7]

Therefore the early education of the infant is critical, for it sets the sail for all future parent-child interrelationships. The counsel is clear.

> The discipline of a human being who has reached the years of intelligence should differ from the training of a dumb animal. The beast is taught only submission to its master. For the beast, the master is mind, judgment, and will. This method, sometimes employed in the training of children, makes them little more than automatons. Mind, will, and conscience, are under the control of another. It is not God's purpose that any mind should be thus dominated. Those who weaken or destroy individuality assume a responsibility that can result only in evil. While under authority, the children may appear like well-drilled soldiers; but when the control ceases, the character will be found to lack strength and steadfastness. Having never learned to govern himself, the youth recognizes no restraint except the requirement of parents or teacher. This removed, he does not know how to use his liberty, and often gives himself up to indulgence that proves his ruin.

> Since the surrender of the will is so much more difficult for some pupils than for others, the teacher should make obedience to his requirements as easy as possible. The will should be guided and molded, but not ignored or crushed. Save the strength of the will; in the battle of life it will be needed.[8]

The striking difference between education that provides a sound basis for future growth, and that which is predictive of psychosocial and spiritual problems, largely depends upon the security of the home.

1. White, *Ministry of Healing*, page 351.
2. Ibid., page 349.
3. White, *Counsels to Parents, Teachers, and Students*, page 107.
4. White, *Ministry of Healing*, pages 375, 376.
5. White, *Counsels to Parents, Teachers, and Students*, page 111.
6. White, *Education*, page 287.
7. See chapter entitled, "Social Education."
8. White, *Education*, pages 288, 289.

Chapter 15
Childhood Education

Childhood, bridging the first two years of infant life with the pre-adult years of adolescence, covers an enormously complex physiological, sociological, intellectual, and spiritual growing period. This is the period to consolidate the quality of education in the infant period, or to attempt to redress serious omissions of that period. It is a time to intensify the efforts to educate the child to clearly reason from cause to effect, especially from the perspective of the principles of God's Word. It is time to teach the child the joy of selfless giving. It is a time to allow guided experimentation in judgment, decisions, and choices. It is time to develop social skills. It is a time to teach responsibility for work skills. It is a time to expand the horizons of the mind, both in content and evaluative skills. And, above all, it is a time to most effectively place before the child the claims of Christ upon his life and service.

It must be emphasized that the effectiveness of parenting in the infant period not only sets the basis for quality psychological adjustment for the child, but tends to influence the quality of parenthood in later years. Unfortunately, poor early parentchild relationships are rarely redressed in later years, and poor habits of early parenting foreshadow continued blundering in later years. Yet for the ones who, in the counsel of the Lord, recognize their earlier failings and seek to change their ineffective methods, there certainly is hope of significant character growth for their children. Parents must commence when the first realization comes to them of their divine ministry, whether it be earlier or later. For "Lo, children are an heritage of the LORD: and the fruit of the womb is His reward" (Psalm 127:3).

What the parent is will determine to a large extent what the child will become. Both father and mother share this responsibility.

> There is a God above, and the light and glory from His throne rests upon the faithful mother as she tries to educate her children to resist the influence of evil. No other work can equal hers in importance. She has not, like the artist, to paint a form of beauty upon canvas, nor, like the sculptor, to chisel it from marble. She has not, like the author, to embody a noble thought in words of power, nor, like the musician, to express a beautiful sentiment in melody. It is hers, with the help of God, to develop in a human soul the likeness of the divine.[1]

> The father should not become so absorbed in business life or in the study of books that he cannot take time to study the natures and necessities of his children. He should help in devising ways by which they may be kept busy in useful labor agreeable to their varying dispositions.

> The father of boys should come into close contact with his sons, giving them the benefit of his larger experience, and talking with them in such simplicity and tenderness that he binds them to his heart. He should let them see that he has their best interests, their happiness, in view all the time. As the priest of the household, he is accountable to God for the influence that he exerts over every member of the family.[2]

It is during childhood that insightful perceptions of self tend to emerge. Both authors have worked in third-world countries where, in terms of material benefits, children have much less than in so-called first-world countries. But it is the authors' observation that there is vastly more deprivation, on the average, for children reared in the latter than in the former. This fact might quickly be evaluated from the following summary which provides hints for healthy child growth in all five facets of life:

PHYSICAL

Parents whose lifestyle is drug free

112

Living in a rural environment

Opportunity for considerable exercise in fresh air and sunshine

Eating of a healthful, high-fiber diet

Learning to work together with parents

EMOTIONAL

Secure, loving management of the child

Consistent discipline of the child

Avoidance of coercive and permissive environments

Avoidance of major time in vicarious experiences

Major experiences in the real world

SOCIAL

Mother in home with child

Close bonding between fathers and sons, and mothers and daughters

Careful monitoring of peer-group companions

INTELLECTUAL

Exploring the real world with parents

Associating activities with concepts

Teaching principles of decision- and choice-making

SPIRITUAL

Regular morning and evening family worship

Teaching the principles of sharing

Making the claims of Christ as attractive as possible

Teaching the principles of life from Bible stories

Living an active witnessing Christian life

The Scriptures emphasize the importance of careful training. Solomon, who perhaps learned the lesson in his own experience, offered this well-known promise to faithful parents:

Train up a child in the way he should go: and when he is old, he will not depart from it (Proverbs 22:6).

PHYSICAL DEVELOPMENT
In an industrial and commercialized world, most children in "advanced" cultures face drug addiction from an early age, even if it begins only with caffeine-based drinks. They live in the cluttered environment of the city, often with little opportunity to enjoy the unstructured exercise that the rural environment offers, largely free from environmental pollution. The preparation of highly fractionated foods has robbed millions of a simple, healthful diet which would strengthen the action of the gastrointestinal system, and help preserve them from the adverse physical and moral influence of a highly refined and processed diet.

Further, apartment living and almost unlimited labor-saving devices have robbed children of the physical, intellectual, and moral virtues of work experience, and have driven them into leisure-time activities which war against the soul.[3] The Christian parent has a God-given obligation to actively seek to provide an environment that will counter every one of these dangers.

EMOTIONAL DEVELOPMENT
Closely interrelated with physical development is emotional maturity. Loving discipline becomes the key to the child's security in present and later life. The child-centered movement has been largely responsible for undiscipline and unhappiness in childhood and later experiences, because of its emphasis upon allowing the child to grow up "naturally." Many Christians, blind to the pernicious influence of such a philosophy, and ignoring the clearest counsel of Scripture, have followed this dangerous counsel to the hurt, and often the eternal ruin, of their children. The concept of the child-centered philosophers is built upon a nonbiblical view of the nature of man. It views man as innately good. If this were so,

the counsel would be sound; but the Scriptures teach that man has a pre-disposition to walk in pathways that are alien to goodness, for they are built upon self-centeredness.

> As it is written, There is none righteous, no, not one (Romans 3:10).

> All we like sheep have gone astray; we have turned every one to his own way (Isaiah 53:6).

> For all have sinned, and come short of the glory of God (Romans 3:23).

> Can the Ethiopian change his skin, or the leopard his spots? then may ye also do good, that are accustomed to do evil (Jeremiah 13:23).

Thus, parental education, training, and loving discipline are essential to the successful development of the child. His happiness is also determined by such an upbringing. Though directed to church leadership, Paul's counsel is surely to all Christians:

> One that ruleth well his own house, having his children in subjection with all gravity (1 Timothy 3:4).

Even more pertinent is Paul's counsel to the Colossians:

> Children, obey your parents in all things: for this is well pleasing unto the Lord (Colossians 3:20).

But let it be emphasized that discipline should not be administered without love. Such severity destroys the self-respect and the independence of the child; just as when love is not expressed within the parameters of sound discipline, great insecurity results.

SOCIAL

It is in childhood that the foundation for behavior and conduct are developed. The parent and teacher have the opportunity to instruct and help educate the child to make wise choices and decisions before the almost overwhelming pressure of peer-group influence has fully matured. In contemporary society, it is critical that this education proceed as early as possible, for the social pressures by peers come frighteningly early into the life of the child.

The importance of the mother in the home cannot be overstressed. We fully agree with the observations of Drs. Provence and Salk:

> "I'm personally convinced that no two parents can rear a child entirely alone," says Dr. Sally Provence of Yale's Child Study Center. "Yet young parents have fewer supports for parenting than ever before—it's either drag the kids along or get a sitter." With the increasing number of young women carving out careers for themselves, some experts see a threat even to the integrity of the nuclear family. "I'd much rather see people not have children at all than leave infants in a day-care center," says Dr. Lee Salk, chief child psychologist at New York Hospital, Comet Medical Center.[4]

The one-parent home is hopelessly unequal to the task of raising children. Yet divorce and separation have almost made this the rule rather than the exception. The selfish irresponsibility that leads to most marital collapses is not only symptomatic of an emotionally unbalanced generation, but tragically will also be reflected in the instability of the next generation.

Yet we have to face the reality that many sincere, godly parents have been thrust into the one-parent situation through no fault of their own. Such need our understanding and support as they struggle against the odds, upheld only by the sustaining power of God. If it is possible for such a parent to obtain support by living with his own parents, this is of significant help. Sometimes the support of the church families can be most helpful also.

Ner Littner has gone at least a good way to define the kind of environment that supplies adequate social-emotional growth.

> "The fortunate child," says Ner Littner of Chicago's Institute of Psychoanalysis, "is the one with good heredity and adequate care provided by two parents who are able to recognize and meet the child's needs in early life, and a minimum of chronic, overwhelming stress situations as the child grows up."[5]

The close bonding of the parents with the children does not lead to the neglect of obedience. Scripture is clear concerning the relationship of children to parents and adults.

> Children, obey your parents in the Lord: for this is right. Honor thy father and mother; which is the first commandment with promise; That it may be well with thee, and thou mayest live long on the earth (Ephesians 6:1–3).

> Likewise, ye younger, submit yourselves unto the elder. Yea, all of you be subject one to another, and be clothed with humility: for God resisteth the proud, and giveth grace to the humble. Humble yourselves therefore under the mighty hand of God, that He may exalt you in due time: casting all your care upon Him; for He careth for you (1 Peter 5:5–7).

Too much encouraged familiarity with adults frequently causes a lack of true reverence for God and for God's representatives. It is especially in early childhood that respect and reverence are developed.

> True reverence for God is inspired by a sense of His infinite greatness and a realization of His presence. With this sense of the Unseen the heart of every child should be deeply impressed. The hour and place of prayer and the services of public worship the child should be taught to regard as sacred because God is there. And as reverence is manifested in attitude and demeanor, the feeling that inspires it will be deepened. . . .

> Reverence should be shown also for the name of God. Never should that name be spoken lightly or thoughtlessly. Even in prayer its frequent or needless repetition should be avoided. "Holy and reverend is His name" (Psalm 111: 9). Angels, as they speak it, veil their faces. With what reverence should we, who are fallen and sinful, take it upon our lips.

> We should reverence God's word. For the printed volume we should show respect, never putting it to common uses, or handling it carelessly. And never should Scripture be quoted in a jest, or paraphrased to point a witty saying. . . .

> Reverence should be shown for God's representatives—for ministers, teachers, and parents who are called to speak and act in His stead. In the respect shown to them He is honored.[6]

The considerable loss of true respect for adults has often led children to indifference in reverence for God. A healthy social development includes an understanding and practice of courtesy for those who are older, and an alertness to the comfort of those in need.

INTELLECTUAL

The education of the mind of the child is a most delicate process. The thought patterns of the child are developed far more by example than by verbal instruction, important though the latter is. Success is always more likely when the child sees modeled in the lives of the parents the principles that they seek to inculcate.

Primary to developing right principles of thinking in the mind of the child is an early familiarity with the great truths of the Bible. The study of the Bible goes well-beyond the development of spiritual values, to the area of providing right principles of thinking.

> An understanding of the revealed will of God, enlarges the mind, expands, elevates, and endows it with new vigor, by bringing its faculties in contact with stupendous truths. If the study of the Scriptures is made a secondary consideration, great loss is sustained.[7]

> As a means of intellectual training, the Bible is more effective than any other book, or all other books combined. The greatness of its themes, the dignified simplicity of its utterances, the beauty of its imagery, quicken and uplift the thoughts as nothing else can. No other study can impart such mental power as does the effort to grasp the stupendous truths of revelation. The mind thus brought in contact with the thoughts of the Infinite can not but expand and strengthen.[8]

David understood the power of the Word in victory over sin.

> Thy word have I hid in mine heart, that I might not sin against Thee (Psalm 119:11).

But, as in intellectual development, so in spiritual, the modeling of the parents is paramount. It makes all the difference if the child recognizes that of utmost importance to the parents are a love of God, a love for His Word, a love for His church, and an earnest witness of their faith.

Often, in the business of life, parents have neglected the centrality of life for the minor issues of everyday concerns. If the child sees faith and implicit trust even in adversity, he, himself, will most likely be attracted to God as his dependence.

The age of childhood bridges the period between the almost total dependency of infancy and the age of increasing independence of adolescence. It represents the time when the individual will begin to evidence the direction of his life. There is still time to "reset the sail" of his life; but, with each increasing year, the task becomes more difficult. The law of primacy is clear—experiences of early life have dominant influence over the experiences of later life.

1. White, *Ministry of Healing,* pages 377, 378.
2. White, *Counsels to Parents, Teachers, and Students,* pages 127, 128.
3. See chapter, entitled "Emotional Education."
4. "Troubled Children: The Quest for Help," *Newsweek,* April 8, 1974.
5. Ibid.
6. White, *Education,* pages 242–244.
7. White, *Fundamentals of Christian Education,* pages 129, 130.
8. White, *Education,* page 124.

Welcome to Chick-fil-A
Barrett Parkway FSU (#00863)
Kennesaw, GA
(770) 421-8650
Operator: Ralph Stephens II
CUSTOMER COPY
7/31/2012 11:30:53 AM
DRIVE THRU

Order Number: 2659576

| 2 | CFA Sand | 5.70 |
| 3 | Fries MD | 4.95 |

	Sub. Total:	$10.65
	Tax:	$0.64
	Total:	$11.29

| | Change | $0.21 |
| | Cash | $11.50 |

Register:2   Tran Seq No: 2659576
Cashier:Abbey

Chapter 16
The Education
of Adolescents

Parents recognize that the adolescent years are usually the last opportunity they have for any course correction in the education of their children. Even then most parents will attest to the fact that it often seems almost too late, once young people have reached the age where they are beginning, increasingly, to make their own individual decisions. Obviously the difficulties that might be experienced with the adolescent are largely the result of past parental training in the child's formative years. Sometimes parents have treated as insignificant, in early childhood, characteristics which become a source of deep concern and worry in the adolescent years. Frequently parents have found their attempts to reverse the results of former home training virtually impossible. However, this must be counterbalanced by the fact that those who have offered a careful and Christ-centered parenting in childhood can often see the youths come through the struggle of adolescence strong and purposeful in their own Christian commitment.

Adolescence is usually considered to be the metamorphosis from childhood to adulthood; and, therefore, we might expect to see, in the same individuals, incidents of childish behavior interspersed with more mature adult behavior. Frequently social and emotional disorders become much more apparent as the individual seeks to discover his own identity. In seeking to find individualized independence, many fail to have established the resources that would enable them to handle even minor stress-inducing situations. The complexity of modern Western society and the extended time of adolescence no doubt exacerbate the problem.

It is usually sometime during the adolescent years that the individual seeks to begin to establish his own value systems. No longer is he prepared to take what his parents and teachers tell him at face value, and sometimes he will violently revolt against what has been part of his early childhood upbringing. This reaction becomes especially true when he is faced with a tug-of-war between the value system of his parents and that of his peer groups. Generally peer-group pressure has an overwhelming dominance, as the individual seeks to be accepted at this level. This fact makes the choice of friends in early years all the more important, for the early establishment of good friends will be a great help in the adolescent years. Conversely, the choice of poor friends inevitably leads to much parental anguish, as the child tends to break away towards the value system of these peers. One cannot but reemphasize the importance of decision-making resources being established in the child long before adolescence. The child who has learned how to make wise decisions stands on vantage ground in contrast with the child who is still grappling with a value system that has not yet been established.

Happy is the child who has already made his decision for Christ. Such individuals, especially in early adolescence, tend to be rare, but they do have the opportunity to strongly stand against the tide of peer-group pressure. Yet sometimes children, who have seemed well-adjusted and have shown a loving relationship with their parents in their formative years, will suddenly show signs of inadequacy, and even rebellion in their early adolescence. Yet this is not a time for parental panic; indeed, it is a time for the continuation of firm but loving management, which will help the youth through this difficult period of time. Indeed, it is important for parents to present a calm and unwavering exterior, while also providing a constant, loving environment that will see the child through the struggles of the adolescent years. Under no circumstances can parents minimize or reduce their God-given principles. Qn the other hand, we have to realize that the child will most certainly have to have the opportunity to make his own decisions, good or bad. But he also must realize that he, himself, must live with the consequences of those decisions.

Parents should continue to positively reinforce the right decisions and actions of their adolescents, helping them to make decisions that are consistent with the highest Christian purposes. Every opportunity should be made available for the child to know that he can still confidently dialogue with both parents. If this communication is cut off, it will not only stifle his development, but it may also lead to a great communication gap which may never be fully bridged. Parents need to carefully evaluate the difference between those differences that might occur which are not of a moral nature from those which are deeply rooted in spiritual law. All the wisdom and energies will be needed to meet those situations which might have a basis in morality.

In the youths' attempt to reach for adulthood, they will often choose arbitrary and undesirable ways of indicating that they are no longer children. Parents can help much by recognizing the increasing independence and maturity of their children. The more this is done, the less likely that the youth will revert to the artificial status symbols such as distinctive dress, makeup, jewelry, smoking, alcohol drinking, drugs, cars, and boyfriend-girlfriend relationships as a sign that they are no longer children. Allowing the adolescent opportunity for responsibility in the home and, indeed, in the church can be of great help here, The youths will eventually be taking the leadership role for God's church, and every effort needs to be made to help them in their major decision-making. The youths need to remember the words of the wise man:

> Remember now thy Creator in the days of thy youth, while the evil days come not, nor the years draw nigh, when thou shalt say, I have no pleasure in them (Ecclesiastes 12:1).

If Satan can possibly weave a web of circumstances around the youths that will make it difficult, if not well-nigh impossible, for them to make subsequent decisions for the Lord, he certainly will do so. It is important to realize that the dominant decision of all other decisions is the decision to serve God. As they have learned in childhood and youth to know the Lord, now they have the responsibility to serve Him.

Indeed, there are four great decisions that are made during life, and it is always best if they are made in the following order:

1. Decision for Christ

2. Preparation for a life calling

3. Choice of a life partner

4. The decision to initiate a new life into the world

If this order is followed, young men and women have the opportunity to grow much closer to the Lord, and to follow much more in His counsel and pathway.

Thou art my trust from my youth (Psalm 71:5).

Such a one has followed the counsel of Paul to Timothy to

Flee also youthful lusts: but follow righteousness, faith, charity, peace, with them that call on the Lord out of a pure heart (2 Timothy 2:22).

The preparation for a life calling is, indeed, a very complex one. Today young people are faced with an inordinate number of choices. Very few at the end of high school have really secured the direction of their life, and even at the end of college, many are still left in uncertainty. How important it is that the youths be taught to make a decision for a life calling rather than for an occupation or a job! It is certainly possible for parents to reduce the tension level for their children in this vital area, if they have helped them to understand that Christ is leading in their lives and that, as they follow His leading, they have nothing to fear. Sometimes they will not know exactly where the Lord is leading; but like Abraham of old, if they follow in God's way they will certainly have nothing to fear. In many cases, it is a matter of encouraging the child to move forward, confident in the Lord's leading. Of course, all educators know that, in general, it is much more likely that a student will persist, and, indeed, will do better should he have a specific goal and objective in mind. How critical it is that parents do not fire their children with unholy ambition—power, prestige, popularity, property, or prosperity. Such egocentric goals will lead to a rivalry and competition which will be self-defeating, and will add to the tension of restless youth. Sister White put it this way:

Be ambitious for the Master's glory.[1]

This purpose, indeed, can be the only valid aim in seeking a life calling.

The decision to choose a life partner will lead to the second most important vow that any human can make, a vow second only to the vow to love, honor, and serve the Lord throughout eternity. It is vital that the young people seek a God-given way to choose a life partner. Present methods are self-destructive. In chapter 21 are some suggestions by which youth can lead toward this most vital decision, in a way that will help them understand the responsibility of marriage, and the joy of joining their lives together in a way that God can honor. Hasty decisions can lead to lifelong misery.

The final decision to initiate a new life is also critical. Often young people choose to be parents before making any other major decisions. Such is catastrophic for their own life, and also for the life of the child brought into the world.

Little has been said about the physiological changes of adolescence. These changes are real and bring with them their own set of expectancies and tensions. But if the energy and the strength of youth can be developed for the purpose of God, what a vast work will be done. It must be kept in mind that it will be largely the youth who will finish the work of God. An awesome responsibility rests upon us to make sure that we do everything we can, so that these adolescents may be among that group who will, with Pentecostal power, take the message of a crucified and soon-coming Saviour to the world. Perhaps the counsel that Jesus gave to the rich young ruler is pertinent here:

> If thou wilt be perfect, go and sell that thou hast, and give to the poor, and thou shalt have treasure in heaven: and come and follow Me (Matthew 19:21).

Paul, during his conversion experience, recognized the vital need for full involvement of his life when he said,

> Lord, what wilt Thou have me to do? (Acts 9:6).

The Lord gave him a mighty ministry, perhaps greater than that of any other apostle. So, too, of the youth today. The Lord is willing to place before them the joy and the privilege of such service. May God help parents to bring this generation to fulfillment.

---

1. White, *Messages to Young People*, page 100.

SECTION D

*Preparation
for a
Life Calling*

Chapter 17
Home-School Education

The home-school movement is gaining tremendous momentum in the United States, and is reaching into some other countries. In many ways this trend seems a reversal from the twentieth-century control of education by the state. What has led to this reversal to home education by many? No doubt the reasons are varied and the psychology is complex, but here are some of the most frequently advanced reasons:

1. Parents are reassessing their God-given responsibilities in the education of their children.

2. Public schools are increasingly reflecting humanistic and non-Christian principles.

3. Social roles in the schools have deteriorated greatly.

4. Peer-group pressures almost always are counterproductive to the Christian parents' goals for their children.

5. Many private schools reflect most of the social ills of the public schools.

6. Costs of private-school education has gone beyond the means of many parents, especially those committed to the mother's playing a full-time role as a homemaker.

7. The academic achievement of students in traditional schools has deteriorated alarmingly.

Typical of the concerns was a telephone call from a non-Seventh-day Adventist stranger to Colin. The woman asked for help should she fail to successfully defend before the school board her reasons for removing her 10-year-old daughter from public school. When asked what her line of defense was she simply said, I do not intend to allow my daughter to go to school to learn to smoke, to drink, to use drugs, to swear, or to be sexually permissive." Her reasons apparently prevailed, for she found no reason to call again for help.

In contrast to the delinquency of some parents in the education of their children around the turn of the century, the home schoolers, almost without exception, are parents with high educational goals for their children. These parents offer a quality of education and academic achievement for their children which goes well-beyond that of their counterparts in the regular school system.

The family environment has always been the center of God-ordained education from Edenic times.

> The system of education established in Eden centered in the family. Adam was "the son of God" (Luke 3:38), and it was from their Father that the children of the Highest received instruction. Theirs, in the truest sense, was a family school.

> In the divine plan of education as adapted to man's condition after the fall, Christ stands as the representative of the Father, the connecting link between God and man; He is the great teacher of mankind. And He ordained that men and women should be His representatives. The family was the school, and the parents were the teachers.[1]

Consistent with this is the following clarification:

> Teaching is as natural for parents as learning is for children. Loving is sharing, and sharing—when it involves ideas—is teaching. You teach as you communicate with your children, as you take care of them, and as you play with them. To a young child the world is new and strange and interesting. As he or she grows a little older it is sometimes frightening. You as a parent are the interpreter. Your child's natural curiosities, fears, needs, and wants are your cues.[2]

Perhaps the best-known authorities on home-school education, Raymond and Dorothy Moore, have this to say:

> No schoolroom can match the simplicity and power of the home in providing three-dimensional, firsthand education. The school, not the home, is the substitute, and its highest function is to complement the family. The family is still the social base, and

must be, if our society is to survive. Let's leave no stone unturned to guarantee the fullest freedom of the home and the rights of parents to determine the education of their children. It is the "stifling" atmosphere of some public and parochial classrooms, says one New Jersey mother, that turns parents back to the flexibility of the home school.

While some parents prefer home education for reasons of religion, moral influences, and absence of ridicule and rivalry, many like this mother see the home as a "more nourishing place for my child to be, where he can make his own decisions, work out his own problems, and go at his own pace under my personal guidance. Here the social pressures are fewer, yet the neighborhood kids love our home." She adds, "My husband and I intend to maintain control of our family. We saw that we were losing it when our son was in kindergarten. We feared the influence he was bringing home before our other children. We are accountable for our kids, so we decided to retain the authority that goes along with this responsibility."[3]

The Christian parents of today share an increasing concern for their divine responsibility in the education of their children. Schools, both public and private, have dangerously deteriorated in providing spiritual, intellectual, social, emotional, and physical education for their children. Those most attracted to the homeschool movement appear to be middle-class people from the more conservative church affiliations, though the movement is by no means limited to these.

Perhaps our most pressing concerns are from those who are members of the Seventh-day Adventist Church. The rapidly increasing attractiveness of the home-school movement for them seems to have two primary bases:

1. The increasing awareness of the end time, in which we live, making greater demands and responsibilities upon parents who have a burden for the salvation of their children, and their preparation for the mission that God has set before them.

2. The developing perception that most Seventh-day Adventist schools are drifting far away from their primary purpose, to offer God-centered education that's pure and untainted by the world.

The authors often hear the cry of consecrated parents who plead to know of a place to which they can entrust the education of their children. Some talk of the increasing worldly entertainment in our schools, others of the lax standards of class management, still others of the erroneous theology being presented to their children. Because these parents are too wise and responsible to turn their children over to secular schools, they see their God-given responsibility as paramount.

Thus in one sense the home-school movement should be a solemn challenge to Seventh-day Adventist schools to return to their upright position of distinction from the world. This is not a call for defensiveness, nor for ridicule of those who have removed their children from formal school, but it is a call to provide authentic Christian education taught by godly, truth-loving teachers.

It will be immediately stated that such education would not be acceptable to many other parents in the church. But surely the Seventh-day Adventist Church must provide only the finest Christian education, opening its doors to all those who desire to benefit by it. There have been those who have sought to decry, and even to report to county authorities, those who choose the home-school route for the education of their children. Such is a sad treatment of sincere Christian parents.

In spite of fears to the contrary, there is much evidence that a wise mother, not necessarily formally educated as a teacher, can educate her children, at least during elementary school years, at a pace and efficiency superior to that of a classroom. The Moores offer support for this.

> At the same time thirteen children from six home school families were tested. All achieved above the 90th percentile, or in the upper 10 percent of the nation. One of Doug Ort's children scored in the 96th percentile, and the other tied with a neighbor's child in the 99th percentile. Recently, thoughtful New York school men have been patient with such home schools.

> Meanwhile, in Nebraska, Lesley Sue Rice gained an average of nearly three years in one year under her high-school-educated mother. And 8-year-old Corinne Johnson of Ridgewood, New Jersey, was excelling in fifth-grade work at home.[4]

It is important to note that most parents who choose the homeschool alternative have noble motives for their children. And who better to achieve these than the child's own mother? By no means do we suggest the home-school for all parents, and certainly not all parents are in a position to offer it. Where quality Christian education is provided, it should be supported. Where it isn't, every Christian effort should be made to seek to achieve it, even while conducting a home-school.

However, there are other considerations. Even for those parents who properly want their children in a classroom environment for much of their formal education, there is still the question of when a child should commence such formal education. In most countries, laws require formal education at 6 to 7 years of age. Many experts disagree that the average child is ready for school at that age. The Moores warn:

> We firmly believe that the greatest teaching talent in the world lies in the warm, responsive and consistent parent whose love makes the needs of his children his highest concern. If anyone disagrees, ask him for his evidence. Parents' daily one-to-one example amounts to master teaching at the highest level.
>
> There are a lot of very good nursery schools, kindergartens, and elementary schools in the world. We have visited many and administered quite a few. Yet there are none whose programs can match education by loving parents of even modest ability, working with their own children in the simplest of homes. And we must not lose this heritage and art.
>
> The family was given to us by the same God in whom our country trusts. On the family rest the pinions of our society. Nevertheless, we have gone a long, long way toward putting it down and substituting parenting-by-state. Now leading social researchers predict the death of our democratic society within a generation. If we are to retrieve it—and our schools—we would do well to look again to God and the home.[5]

For the first eight to ten years at least—until their values are formed—most parents, even average parents, are by far the best people for their children. And those that are not, usually can and should be. To be sure, there are areas of child care in which others can outdo parents—such as physicians, nurses, and specialty teachers in music and the arts. But in general the best teacher or care-giver cannot match a parent of even ordinary education and experience, Dr. Marcelle Geber's studies in Uganda proved that even tribal mothers who did not know how to read or write reared children who were more intellectually and socially alert and secure by Western standards than well-educated mothers. The difference? Tribal mothers were close to their children. So-called higher class mothers tended to share the care of their children with others.[6]

Of course what the Moores say is consistent with divine counsel.

Do not send your little ones away to school too early. The mother should be careful how she trusts the molding of the infant mind to other hands. Parents ought to be the best teachers of their children until they have reached eight or ten years of age. Their schoolroom should be the open air, amid the flowers and birds, and their textbook the treasure of nature. As fast as their minds can comprehend it, the parents should open before them God's great book of nature. These lessons, given amid such surroundings, will not soon be forgotten.[7]

Whenever possible, opportunity should be taken for mothers to be the teachers in these early years. The authors recognize that because of the nature of some circumstances, some children will best be educated in a school environment. The children of the one-parent homes have often come into this category where, for very serious reasons, the mother is unsuited to the task. But it would seem that these would be the exceptions rather than the rule. Even in these circumstances, whenever possible, a number of families might group together with one suitable mother providing the home-school guidance.

The church will still need to provide, in many places, education for younger children, but this education will be at a much reduced level. In turn this will help diminish the costs of church-school operations. The home-school movement is seen to be a movement that is here to stay; and, in spite of governmental and other sources of opposition, the increasing evidence of its success will secure its future. Seventh-day Adventist parents need to consider this matter intelligently and prayerfully. In the judgment they will account for the education of their children.

1. White, *Education*, page 33.
2. Wade, Theodore E., Jr., et al., *School at Home*, page 23.
3. Moore, Raymond and Dorothy, *Home Grown Kids*, pages 26, 27.

4. Ibid, page 24.
5. Ibid., pages 12–14
6. Ibid., pages 32, 33.
7. White, *Fundamentals of Christian Education,* pages 156, 157.

Chapter 18
Elementary Education

While, unquestionably, the home is the first and most important influence upon the child, it is normal and consistent with Christian principles for children to be provided with more formal education. There can be no question that the church has a vital responsibility in the education of its children; however, such education can never supersede the education given by the parents. As has been indicated previously,[1] the primary responsibility in education is that of the parents; thus, the role of the school is to second the educational role of the parents, not to supplant it nor to supersede it.

Ideally, the Christian home will be such a place that the boys and girls have had the maximum opportunity to learn about God and to see Christian modeling by their parents, in a way that will fit them for a Christian school that's established upon the authentic principles that God has given. Yet, in reality, we have to recognize that few children today have come from the highest quality Adventist homes, and that, indeed, few elementary schools offer an education patterned upon the principles that God has given. It is difficult to know how to remedy this situation. It is common for the parents to blame the schools for their inadequacies, and for teachers to blame the parents.

There are those who argue that the school must reflect the eclecticism in our church, but this course is not consistent with the God-given purpose of our schools. Many school administrators and teachers feel that they are duty-bound to offer an education that is consistent with the patterns of Christian life in the community. This concept has left many fine, dedicated Christian parents in a dilemma. These parents have provided the finest home environment possible, and the kind of school that they have in mind for their children is equally consistent with God's pattern. Yet it is very difficult for them to find such schools that are denominationally operated. This fact has led many parents to seek self-supporting schools which are established upon these patterns. But, even here for some, there is a conflict. Some of these self-supporting schools, though upholding the highest standard of Christian commitment, have appeared to the parents to have presented these standards from a rather arbitrary and legalistic perspective. There are some schools, however, that both uphold the highest standards and yet provide the framework of education for the students in an understanding, yet growth-inducing, environment. More such schools seem to be developing, and these are receiving more and more support. But surely these cannot supply the needs all around the world; and, indeed, the time is well-overdue for reformation to take place in denominationally operated schools. It must be conceded that this reformation will be very difficult. It is not uncommon for schools to fall towards the lowest denominator of those who are placing pressure upon them. It is obvious that the less converted tend to exert more pressure than the converted. Thus, the steps of compromise tend to be achieved much more readily than the steps of reformation.

The whole issue is compounded by the fact that few, even of committed parents, have a real understanding of what God's true principles are for Christian education; and many have, themselves, received such an education that they are inclined to believe that the full implementation of the divine model would tend to cause fanaticism. Further, they are sometimes placed in a quandary by those who vigorously argue that the school should take the children where they are. While, of course, there is some truth in this, it must be quickly pointed out that the only way to uplift children is to provide the fullest, most authentic Christian education possible. Indeed, Christ the Master Teacher is our pattern in this endeavor. He ever upheld the highest and most complete standard of His Father, yet He also showed compassion and understanding for the fallen ones. Perhaps nothing demonstrates this truth more clearly than the experience of Mary Magdalene:

> And Jesus said unto her, Neither do I condemn thee: go, and sin no more (John 8:11).

While showing love and acceptance of Mary, Christ, nevertheless, pointed to the only way in which she could have the fuller life leading to real meaning and real purpose.

When the child enters school, he is already very set in his ways. The years that he experienced at home have made a profound impact upon him, indeed, greater than any subsequent impact can make. The character has already been substantially formed. The issues of selfishness or selflessness have forged significant habit patterns in his life. This fact does not mean, of course, that it is too late to do anything, but it does make the role of the teacher a challenging one.

A society where most countries require children to be in school before their optimal readiness has provided a very great dilemma for the teacher. Colin well-remembers his early experience when parents decided that their 4-year-old was ready for school. The lad soon proved how unready he was, and had to be returned to his home environment.

Indeed, the counsel that it is usually wiser for the mother to be the teacher until the age of 8 or 10 has borne the test of time. The 5- or 6-year-old is socially too immature to handle the group relationship; and he rarely is psychologically, physically, or cognitively ready for the school environment. It is unfair for the immature child to be away from his parents, especially his mother, for such long periods of time. Often the activities he is required to perform are taxing upon his yet immature physical resources. Sometimes the child, who has appeared relatively well-adjusted at home, will show strong evidences of maladjustment once he reaches the school situation. This reaction frequently leads the parent to conclude that the teacher is ineffective or does not understand his child. Yet it is often possible that the parents have indulged the child; and, thus, he feels fairly comfortable and rewarded. But once he reaches the group situation of the classroom where he is no longer the center of attention, and no longer is able to have his whims reinforced, he finds the situation distasteful; and, consequently, he exhibits evidence of maladaptive behavior and often antisocial patterns. It is usually difficult to convince the parents that their training has been the problem rather than the lack of understanding in the teacher.

Further, as the child reaches school, he has pressures on him that he has not experienced before. For example, he may have been well-accepted for his pleasant personality and his good relationships with his parents. But now he is confronted with pressures of academic achievement that were not upon him before; and, should he prove mediocre in performance, often the anxiety level of the parents is raised, which is translated into negative interactive relationships with the child. And so a new dimension comes upon him. How important it is that parents do not place stress upon him; and, especially, that they do not compare the performance of the child with that of another child in the family. Neither should they compare him with some other relative, or, indeed, with any other child in the classroom. The whole purpose of Christian education is to avoid comparison, and to make it clear that the child is only expected to do the best that he can. God is a God who recognizes the difference in abilities and talents. It is obvious that the student who gets a B, when indeed his abilities would allow an A, is dishonoring God in a way that is not true of the child who through genuine effort achieves a C.

It is inevitable that from time to time the initiative for educational reformation will vary. In some places it will be the teacher or teachers who will initiate. At other times it will be the pastor or the parents. Happy, and predictably successful, will be the situation when teachers, pastors, and the majority of parents are involved in this reformation. It is the experience of the authors, however, that this will rarely be the case. Often the least successful in effecting a return to fundamental Christian education will be the teacher, if he does not have the support of the parents and the pastor. It will frequently be argued that he is rigid and even fanatical. Often he is faced with a choice, to transfer, to drop out of denominational employment, or, alternatively, to modify his approach to placate those who are not convinced of the necessity for these reformatory changes, and indeed are in opposition to and possibly hostile to them. The teacher has to make an evaluation of how deep his convictions are. This soulsearching can be very difficult indeed. Likewise if it is the pastor who is seeking these reforms, he too can be faced with unbelievable difficulties. He can be accused of interfering with the school, and failing to support the teachers. This situation can also bring him into crossfire with his parishioners; and, very likely, his alternatives are similar to those of the teacher who seeks reform.

Perhaps those who have the greatest opportunity to effect reform are indeed the parents of the children in the school. But, even here, there are hazards. In this age of loyalty, it is most likely that the conference educational department will feel obliged to support the teacher who is resistant to change. The pastor will probably feel a similar obligation. Even if there is only a small vocal minority of parents who, because of their own worldliness or ignorance, are resistant to change in the school, then it is very likely that the majority will not be able to achieve their desired goals. It is the experience of the authors that where two of these three influences—teachers, pastor, or parents—are fully prepared to implement reformation, they will probably succeed, albeit with considerable opposition. It is likely that, irrespective of the perspective of the conference education department, if the strengths are enough and the unity apparent, the department will probably agree to the necessary changes. We might hasten to say that not all education department personnel oppose change, for there are some who themselves have a commitment to reformation, and will facilitate it wherever possible.

We would advise that much broad-scale education take place before reformation be initiated. Many people will oppose, not because of worldliness or indifference but because of ignorance; and, therefore, it is important to bring as many as possible to a knowledge of the true principles of God. Obviously an important starting point is the study of the counsels that God has given in books such as *Education; Fundamentals of Christian Education; Counsels to Parents, Teachers, and Students;* and *Counsels on Education.* Of course, knowledge will not guarantee support; but, at least, it will help those who are honestly seeking to follow God's way to view education from the divine perspective. It is also important that as wide a group as possible be involved in the planning and changes that are to be made, and full understanding and reasons be given. Further, it is essential that the students in the school be brought into a deeper understanding, for often they will be more readily convinced than even their parents. Above everything else, those who are most deeply convicted will need to meet together regularly for prayer, to pray specifically for the needs, recognizing that God is even more interested in this reformation than they are.

It will be readily understood that reformation will more likely take place in a smaller than in a larger school. It has been the experience of the authors that large elementary schools will have a sizeable percentage of staff that will band together against reformation.

There has to be some sympathy for the perspective of the teacher. The teacher has not been educated in most instances in the true principles of Christian education, nor has his own education been along these lines. The natural tendency is to teach as one has been taught and as one has been trained. Thus any direction at reformation can be perceived by the teachers as an indictment upon their performance and their ability.

Once threatened, it is unlikely that their support will be obtained. It is our suggestion that those, who are committed to seek the reformation that God would want, determine in a systematic way what steps must be taken and when these should be taken. Then the return to the true principles of God can be effected in a way which will not go too far ahead of the people and their understanding.

Because it is during elementary school that most young people are baptized, the kind of education provided there has to maximize the spiritual goals to be achieved. Above everything it should be recognized that no teacher can be forced into a pattern of true education. If a teacher feels unsupportive of the reformation that is desired by the church, then in mutual understanding it ought to be decided that that teacher go to an area where his philosophy and concepts are accepted.

Once the reformation in the school has been achieved, there is no guarantee that it will continue. It will take God-given vigilance, and the most careful selection of staff for the reformation to be perpetuated. Perhaps the direction of this reformation is best summed up in the following statement:

> Students will come to the school who have no definite purpose, no fixed principles. They will have no realization of the claims of God upon them; but they are to be inspired with courage, to be awakened to their responsibilities, that they may have high aims, desire to improve their talents, and increase their knowledge. They must be taught to appreciate their opportunities, that they may thirst for knowledge and become examples in industry, sobriety, and punctuality.[2]

True Christian education in the elementary school does not call for lowering standards to accommodate the unconverted, but rather the presentation of true Christian principles in the spirit of Christ, so that each child may have maximal opportunity to experience the fullness of the claims of Christ upon his life and service.

1. See the chapter entitled, "Home-School Education."
2. White, *Bible Echo and Signs of the Times,* September 1, 1892.

Chapter 19
Academy and High School Education

The age of entry into high school around the world varies from country to country, but it generally falls between the ages of 12 and 14. These years represent the age of early adolescence, that period of time when young people are seeking to assert their independence, and to make decisions which will be of ultimate consequence to their future life. The Christian parents are often faced with a very difficult dilemma concerning the education of their children. In North America, where the tendency is to commence high school or academy at about age 14, a large percentage of Seventh-day Adventists have solved this problem by sending their children to boarding academies. In most other parts of the world, there is much greater reluctance to do so; because, in many countries, the high school experience commences in the seventh grade or about age 12. However, even in the United States and Canada, there is a genuine dilemma that parents face. Is a 14-year-old mature and stable enough in his own value system and decision-making processes to leave the critical influence of the home? It can be argued that the Bible is replete with examples of those who left home at an early age, and yet became great leaders for God. Obviously Samuel and Moses readily come to mind. Moses' experience is all the more remarkable; in that after the age of 12, he was in a heathen environment, totally inimical to the education that he had received from his mother. It can hardly be denied, however, that today we face a complicated society, perhaps more confusing than any in the previous history of the world. And the influence of the home becomes of paramount significance.

It is most unlikely that even the best academies with the most dedicated faculty can adequately substitute for the role of a true Christian home. It must be considered that the majority of young people at 14, even from good homes, have not made final, irrevocable decisions to follow Christ, albeit they may be baptized. At this time, peer-group pressure also becomes exceptionally significant, and it would be naive to believe that all other students at the boarding academy will have a positive and productive spiritual influence. It is the belief of the authors that, for most youths, it is far better for them to be with their parents until at least college age.[1] The dilemma is heightened, however, by the fact that many times people live in communities where there is no Seventh-day Adventist day academy or high school available. Some have solved this problem by moving within range of such a day academy for the benefit of their children, but it would be fair to say that many find that solution most difficult, if not impossible, because of the circumstances of their life and occupation. The situation is further complicated by the fact that most of our day academies are located in centers where there are large Adventist communities. Frequently these have developed into "Jerusalem" centers, where the moral and spiritual influence is low. It has often been recognized that it is more difficult for young people to grow into full Christian maturity when they are bombarded by the temptations of the children of fellow Adventists than it is when their bombardment comes from non-Adventist sources. Adventist centers are especially vulnerable to negative influences.

A review of God's counsel, whether it be in terms of hospitals, churches, or schools, always leans towards the development of small institutions. It would seem that the most satisfactory solution to this problem would be the establishment of small academies, scattered widely, so that as many as possible of our young people would be within range of such a day academy. This plan would allow the children the opportunity to continue to grow within the protection of the home, and thus help the youth through the awkward and difficult age of peer-group pressure. Some may quickly reason that such a small school would be, at a great disadvantage for a number of reasons, especially because of a lack of facilities and wide-ranging options from which the student can choose; however, the most important consideration is the spiritual and moral environment in which our children are educated.

Evidence points to the fact that smallness in nowise will necessarily bring a disadvantage. The authors, themselves, spent their last seven years of schooling at the Newcastle Adventist School, when the total enrollment from first grade to the end of high school was at or under 50 students. There were those who pressed our parents to send us to the large, well-equipped, and highly-qualified staff of the Newcastle Boys' High School. It was argued that we would be at a very grave disadvantage for our future careers if we stayed at the small Christian school. Indeed, there were those, even among the ministry who removed their children from the Adventist school to send them to the highly-reputed state school. The awesome carnage in defection from the church is more than ample testimony to the lack of wisdom of such a decision. More than this, the warnings of well-meaning church members to our parents proved erroneous; and we are ever grateful for our mother's reply, "We want our boys to have a Christian education."

Hard statistical evidence that Colin accumulated while a college president showed that without exception the students comparable academy performance were at a significant advantage at the college level when they had come from smaller academies. Never were the larger boarding academies able to produce students who could academically perform at the level of those who had come from the smaller, less crowded, but more poorly equipped academies. Perhaps this is due to the fact that staff was able to provide careful care and attention for students in the smaller academy with a family-like situation, which was less available in the larger academies.

Some years ago a similar statistical study at the University of Sydney, Australia, showed that though the performance of those Adventist students who had come from the small Adventist high schools had been no better than that of those who had come from the large and highly sophisticated state high schools, their performance at the University of Sydney was significantly better, statistically. These are important findings, the results of which should not be overlooked. Perhaps, in the latter case, the greater spiritual commitment, and the ability to learn to work together and yet more independently in a multigrade organization, that was experienced by those in a small Adventist school, may have been a far better preparation for post-secondary work than the stronger spoon-feeding that often comes in the larger institution.

There is another point of consideration. Contrary to the beliefs of many, an academy that is carefully designed, and can enroll a specified number of students, will be financially more viable than a large academy. The per-student cost of operation will be much lower. As Adventist educators, we have frequently blundered in this area. We have rejected counsel that we should not count success in numbers.

> To lower the standard in order to secure popularity and an increase of numbers, and then to make this increase a cause of rejoicing, shows great blindness. If numbers were an evidence of success, Satan might claim the pre-eminence; for in this world his followers are largely in the majority. It is the degree of moral power pervading a school that is a test of its prosperity. It is the virtue, intelligence, and piety of the people composing our schools, not their numbers, that should be a source of joy and thankfulness.[2]

Often it has been argued that the funds being used to build new buildings will not affect operations, for they are, indeed, separate funds coming from capital appropriations. But such an argument is shallow. Obviously we have but one major source for funds, operational or capital, and that is from our church membership. But more than this, it is a well-known fact that every building costs, in operation, about 5 percent of what its capital investment is. Two percent is in depreciation; and, then, there are the costs of insurance, maintenance, lighting, heating, cooling, and janitorial services, which all add to the burden of operation; thus a million-dollar building will cost about $50,000 per year to operate. With the fluctuation of enrollment, institutions are often left with crippling financial burdens leading to the collapse of those institutions, or at least to their becoming millstones around the necks of conferences.

Attention should also be given to the tremendous additional cost that is involved in administrating a large academy or college. By the time assistants and deputies are added and committees making the same decisions are enlarged, the administrative costs escalate very rapidly. Academies, designed for about 60 students, each with a carefully chosen staff, and with quality industries to help support the finances and to provide the basis for the work-study program, will operate in a manner that would allow many more of our youths to enjoy the privilege of attending a Christian school.

There is still, of course, the situation of options. It is true that, in a small school, there is no way that the options can be as great as they are in a large school; and, for some, this fact will create considerable concern. It can be a disadvantage of a small school; yet, if there is a well-balanced and varied required curriculum, in which the students learn those essential disciplines and practical arts for life, the narrower range of options need not be a very great disadvantage. Often a school is faced with great difficulty in its optional offerings; thus, the teacher is frequently required to teach areas in which he himself is not specifically educated, and often the quality of optional courses is inferior. In any case, it is the view of the authors that this is a small price to pay for the other overwhelming advantages of a small-school environment.

The high school period is, indeed, the age of decision.[3] Clearly the spiritual and moral factors of education need to be paramount. This responsibility should not be left to the Bible teacher and the religious exercises alone, but should permeate the totality of the curriculum. The modeling of home life is important, for some of the students will enter these academies without having experienced a united Christian home. It must be recognized that for many students this opportunity for Christian influence will be the last that they will have, for some will not proceed to college. Thus it behooves the teacher to do all in his power to place the claims of Christ in the most attractive way before the student. It must be the goal of every teacher that no student will leave the academy without first having surrendered his life to the dominance of the love of Christ.

But there are other areas that need serious consideration in the Christian school. We have often done little better than the public-school system in helping our young people to have the kind of education that will best prepare them for subsequent life. Today colleges and universities face a dilemma. So many of the students, applying as graduates from high schools and academies, are at such a low level, especially in the fundamental skills of English, science, and mathematics. This situation is especially chronic in countries like the United States where, unlike many other countries where the spiral system dominates, the block system applies, making it possible for students to escape the more essential areas of education by taking soft options. Because of our commitment to educate for the finishing of the work of God, we cannot be deficient in these areas. By allowing our students, and sometimes encouraging them, to take the soft options, we place them at a terrible disadvantage. And we deny them the education that God has planned.

> The youth should be taught to aim at the development of all their faculties, the weaker as well as the stronger. With many there is a

disposition to restrict their study to certain lines, for which they have a natural liking. This error should be guarded against. The natural aptitudes indicate the direction of the lifework, and, when legitimate, should be carefully cultivated. At the same time it must be kept in mind that a well-balanced character and efficient work in any line depend, to a great degree, on that symmetrical development which is the result of thorough, all-round training.[4]

There is a special emphasis upon the basic building-block courses, which underlie many of the disciplines that the student may subsequently choose.

So long as the great purpose of education is kept in view, the youth should be encouraged to advance just as far as their capabilities will permit. But before taking up the higher branches of study, let them master the lower. This is too often neglected. Even among students in the higher schools and the colleges there is great deficiency in knowledge of the common branches of education.[5]

This counsel emphasizes the importance of developing the basic skills in English communication, both written and oral. These will allow the effective witness of the gospel. Simple mathematics and calculational skills, in spite of calculators and computers, are still essential, and form the basis of effective study in the sciences. There are also, in this modern age of technology, industrialization and health care, the need for a strong high-school background in the science areas, especially in chemistry. Yet so many who subsequently seek to pursue a course of study in one of these fields have avoided taking courses in them in academy, accentuating the anxiety in college, and sometimes depriving the individual of the opportunity to reach the goals that he has established. There should be no encouragement for young people in Christian academies to look for the easiest way through. Rather the emphasis should be upon that personalized help that will enable even the weakest students to achieve success in these valuable disciplines.

In North America, in yet another area, we have capitulated, at least in part, to worldly principles. Rather than the senior year being a serious and concentrated final preparation for the work or study ahead, it is frequently a year of socialization. It is common for students to leave only the easier courses for the last year, so that they can enjoy the social benefits of the senior year experience. We cannot uncritically accept the oft-repeated claim that socialization is one of the most important goals of academy life. Of course, social interaction is of vital importance. But the type of activity provided is rarely uplifting, not being representative of the more mature social interrelationships that characterize the life of the true Christian. The emphasis of the senior year should be much more upon deepening spiritual relations and ministry skills than upon cheap socialization, which often incorporates much in the way of worldly entertainment. The authors strongly recommend a serious look at the senior year in the North American academies, so that a redirection and emphasis different from that of the world may be established.

Often the academy situation has not been helped by the emphasis in the Bible classes of recent years. Two areas particularly trouble the authors.

1. The great emphasis upon sociology and psychology. This is a time when our young people need, above everything else, to know the four great pillars of our faith—the Law of God, the Sabbath, the Sanctuary, and the State of the Dead. They need to know them so that they will not be deceived by the dissonant voices who are claiming that the Adventist pillars are not biblical truths. While it is important for our young people to know all the great doctrines of the Bible, it is obvious that in the final testing days ahead they will be challenged concerning the coming of Jesus, baptism by immersion, the Godhead, and the sacrifice of Christ. Many members of other denominations accept these. But on the four pillars for which Satan has such contempt they will need to give an account. Therefore, none should leave our academies without fully being able, for their own benefit, and for their witness to others, to know the biblical basis of each truth.

2. Many times the students have been given Bible workbooks with no final answers, but have been allowed to dialogue the issues from the depths of their inexperience. Thus the students come to believe more and more in an existential approach to religion, in which their opinions are as good as those of the next, and they are not led to find final, irrevocable answers from the Word of God. This fact is one of the reasons why so few now can accept as final a "Thus saith the Lord." It has been argued that this kind of presentation is important to develop the reasoning skills of the young people. The authors question this assertion, believing that the answers of

the Word of God are critical to valid Christian living. Indeed it has been found that those receiving this kind of doctrinal education become individuals least able to form firm and valid conclusions from their study of God's Word, for they are lost in a world of uncertainty.

Those who have been observers of our academies over an extended period of time have realized a very dramatic change in the method of discipline. There is no question that in many cases discipline in the past has been arbitrary and almost legalistic. However, today an opposite trend is, apparently, one of permissiveness. Whereas the first seemed to emphasize the justice of God, the second is emphasizing the love of God. Both trends are detrimental to the spiritual growth of young people. The marriage of justice and mercy is critical, Today students are sometimes tamely reprimanded for things that formerly would have led to immediate expulsion, such as the use of drugs, sexual promiscuity, alcohol and tobacco usage. While the erring student should be given every opportunity to be restored, the morale of the school and the influence upon the student body demands that students who are guilty of serious violations, in moral or spiritual conduct, must be removed from the school. This removal should be done in the most loving way, with the indication that the student has the right to return. Above everything, once a student has been given a final chance, should he become delinquent again, it is of serious demoralization to a student body, if action is not taken. No course of action taken presents a wrong view of God, indicating that sin is not sinful, as indeed it is. The student, of course, must realize that the door has never been closed finally, and that when he has come into a deeper and fuller relationship with the Lord, it will be possible for him to reapply and be restored in the school. To act in a way, however, which does not show the deep consequences of sin is to deny the youth opportunity to understand true cause-and-effect relationships in the spiritual life.

Today is a difficult time in our academies. There is much immorality and spiritual declension among the students. Yet there are those also in our academies that are showing the deeper and fuller commitment of their lives to the Lord. Often our efforts have almost ignored the needs of these students in favor of the others. Frequently an early disciplinary action will have profound positive influence throughout life; whereas the continual indulgence of wrong will lead to a lifelong enslavement to sin. Surely our high schools and academies have a momentous task before them. We must spare no effort to bring them back to the full principles by which God would have them operate. Expulsion must be reserved for the most serious problems of discipline, for it commonly leaves significant scars upon the child. The goal of the child's redemption must ever determine the actions of school administrators.

> One thing I wish you to understand, that I have not been in harmony with the expelling of students from the school, unless human depravity and gross licentiousness make it necessary, that others shall not be corrupted.[6]

1. See chapter entitled, "The Education of Adolescents."
2. White, *Testimonies for the Church,* Volume 6, page 143.
3. Russell and his wife have experienced the pain of sending their sons to boarding academy.
4. White, *Education,* pages 232, 233.
5. Ibid., page 234.
6. White, *Fundamentals of Christian Education,* page 277.

Chapter 20
College Education

Persistent financial crises confronted by most Seventh-day Adventist colleges have caused many educators, as well as laymen, to re-evaluate the direction and the purpose of Seventh-day Adventist post-secondary education. Many unions in North America and overseas divisions are finding the financial strain increasingly difficult to handle. Yet all recognize the importance of college education to the task of preparing the youth of the church for their distinctive roles in denominational service. Indeed, it is noted that, in almost all areas of the world, the first level of education that has been commenced is at the college level. It has been considered of prime importance that there be a well-trained, qualified group of workers to proclaim the Advent faith.

We have done much to follow the counsel that God has given, to have colleges in a wide range of countries in the world, where a high percentage of students can study within the realm of their own culture.

> To supply the need of laborers, God desires that educational centers be established in different countries where students of promise may be educated in the practical branches of knowledge and in Bible truth. As these persons engage in labor, they will give character to the work of present truth in the new fields. They will awaken an interest among unbelievers and aid in rescuing souls from the bondage of sin. The very best teachers should be sent to the various countries where schools are to be established, to carry on the educational work.[1]

However, like the situation that exists in our academies, we have allowed our colleges to become too large. We have much counsel upon this. When Battle Creek College had approximately 1,000 students, Ellen White indicated it was at least three times the maximum size that it should be.[2] And following the giving of this counsel, when the college was shifted to Berrien Springs for the establishment of Emmanuel Missionary College, the board voted that it should not accept more than 250, or at the maximum 300, students. No doubt this action was in response to the counsel that God had given.

There are a number of reasons why our colleges would benefit from being small. First, the opportunity for teachers to work closely with students and to get to know them well has unquestionable advantage in every facet of their lives, especially spiritually and intellectually. It was the experience of Colin, while president of Columbia Union College, that at the end of four years, he was shaking hands with some students whose faces he could not even recognize. This is an unfortunate situation. It is sometimes argued that in the larger schools, while not every teacher has the opportunity to know every student, there is still a situation whereby departmental chairmen and advisers do come into close contact with the students. But experience testifies to the fact that, in a large school, never is it possible to have the same close relationship with all students.

The second value of developing many small schools is that they provide college education within closer range of the homes of the potential students. Under these circumstances, it stands to reason that a greater percentage of our young people would find themselves in Christian colleges.

Third, decentralization allows for the witness of the college to be much more effectively experienced.

> If some of our large educational institutions were broken up into smaller ones, and schools established in various places, greater progress might be made in physical, mental, and moral culture. . . . The large amount of means invested in a few localities should be used in providing facilities for a wider field so that many more students could be accommodated.[3]

If we had followed this counsel, and many small colleges were located around the world in which the developed community outreach program had been established, tremendous results would have taken place.

There are those, however, who, in spite of the clarity of God's counsel, argue very strongly for the centralization of higher education. They argue that, indeed, we have too many colleges of higher education for the church to support, particularly in North America. They should be limited to five, even perhaps to two institutions. Such point to other religious organizations in support of their viewpoint. For example, the Mormons with their highly influential Brigham Young University are often cited. But the authors believe that this argument is contrary to divine counsel, and as such, contrary to the goals of Christian higher education.

Once again, it is argued that the diversity of courses presently offered in our colleges would not be possible in smaller institutions; however, the smaller institutions could be a reality if we were to consider two areas. One is the fact that our foundation principles provided for education specifically in the area of Christian service. Two is the requirement that every college would offer only specified majors. In respect to the latter, the Board of Higher Education of North America, in recent years, has attempted, with only limited success, to reduce the number of competing majors offered by colleges in North America. It would take careful planning and full decision-making, but this end could possibly be achieved. It might well be argued that institutions have grown so large that now it is well-nigh impossible for them to be moved, or for us to establish according to divine principle. Most properties, however, are in areas of high value and, with divine assistance, could be sold in such a way that a number of smaller institutions could be established consistent with the counsel of God. Those, who believe that size is the basic criterion of influence, may have overlooked the fact that the influence of a small college, closely following the model that God has given, will attract much greater attention than that of an institution much larger but more traditional in format. This has been the experience of Colin who, having served in a number of larger more traditional denominational colleges, and also at Weimar College and Hartland College, has seen the much greater impact of the latter, not only upon the Adventist community but also upon the community at large.

There is no question that, as we follow God's pattern, great interest is created among educators in the world at large, with an influence vastly beyond the size of the institution.

While there is validity to the argument that Christian higher education should be provided for as wide a range of young people as possible, the tendency has been more and more to offer that kind of education which is only marginally different from that of the world. It certainly is true that whatever discipline might be chosen, whatever calling might be followed, it can be an avenue through which the student can find witness to the Lord. But if these courses become more and more secular, and in the advisement of our students, we uphold motivations which are in conflict with the selfless life of Jesus, then, indeed, we have no right to be offering such courses, nor to be spending denominational funds for the training of these students. Whatever the major, it should be so designed that it can give the maximal opportunity for every student to find his first role in outreach witness for the Lord.

Another area of concern is that of extended theoretical training. Today it is common for young people to spend 16, if not 20, years in study programs without having any significant period of time in the practical spheres of life, to reinforce what they are learning. This, indeed, is poor education, and one which cannot offer to the student the best preparation for life. The introduction, some time ago, of the student missionary program certainly offers an opportunity for students to break their education in the middle of their college schooling. This program has been invaluable to many students in focusing their lives and adding depth to their preparation. The situation is exacerbated, however, by the fact that only a small percentage of students take the opportunity to engage in an extended and ongoing witness program during their school life. Clearly it is advantageous to students if there is, as an integral part of the program, an outreach ministry. Further, if they have the opportunity to take some extended period of time from their studies to develop their God-given talents in some branch of worthwhile endeavor, it is helpful. This plan becomes exceedingly essential if we recognize that our purpose is not only to train Christian workers, but to train Christian leaders. While there is an advantage in training someone to be a Christian follower, and some benefits will accrue, it is obvious that if we educate leaders then their influence will be vastly greater. We recognize that God's remnant church will always be a small church, that only a few will be ready to receive the power of the Holy Spirit; therefore, it is essential that as many as possible have the fullest development of their leadership capabilities. This is another reason why our schools should be small. There is absolutely no way that leaders can be mass-produced. The opportunity for leadership responsibilities in committees and in various student activities is not possible for more than a small range of students in a large institution. But in a small institution it is possible for every student to develop these talents.

Some may argue that the student association is the obvious place in which to develop the talents of the students and their leadership roles. Over the years these associations, which were established to fit with the concepts of accrediting bodies, have often militated against the concepts of true leadership growth. Unfortunately, the very nature of such organizations, especially as they are compared with those in secular institutions, tends to divide the students from the faculty. It is obvious that a student association executive feels his responsibilities to represent the needs and the desires of the students. Often in the past, particularly in the 1960s and early 1970s, the student associations proved to be pressure groups, used to erode Christian principles in the college. Colin has been associated with denominational colleges, with and without student associations. It is his experience that by far the best relationship existed when there was no student association. This fact did not mean that the students did not have a full and responsible role in the government of the school. Indeed, in many ways it was possible to bring them closer into the administrative responsibilities. This result has certainly been the case in Weimar College and in Hartland College. But it has always been in a responsible and cooperative venture, where students and staff work together for the fulfillment of God's purpose in the school. Often the student association newspapers have been an embarrassment to the church; and it seems difficult, if not well-nigh impossible, to control their emphases. Such has never been a problem where student associations do not exist; for the papers represent not simply the voice of the students but the voice of the college as a whole.

One of the great dilemmas that faces our colleges today is the problem of the worldly training of professors. While it is true that Ellen White indicated that a few well-chosen young men might be given the responsibility of receiving an education in worldly institutions, so that they might come back to teach in our schools, she has the strongest condemnation against bringing this worldly education into the schools.

> There are some who, having secured this worldly education, think that they can introduce it into our schools. But let me tell you that you must not take what the world calls the higher education and bring it into our schools and sanitariums and churches. We

need to understand these things. I speak to you definitely. This must not be done.[4]

Unfortunately a flood door has opened. The pressures have often been so that the degree has been more emphasized than the spiritual preparation. Of course, it must always be recognized that solid quality academic information must be available from all Christian teachers. But this need is subservient to the teacher's total commitment to Christ and to the principles of the kingdom of God. We now face a situation where it would be difficult to believe that any one of our colleges does not have a significant number of teachers who, because of their worldly thinking and inconsistency with the principles of the Seventh-day Adventist Church, should no longer be teaching there. Yet it has been found exceedingly difficult to rid the institutions of these professors; however, this bold task confronts administrators. It will always be argued that such treatment is unfair and unkind to the professors concerned; but, indeed, they do not have the right to continue to present that which is inconsistent with God's church, to the students entrusted to them. The kindest and the fairest response is to ask such to discontinue. Until this separation takes place, our institutions of higher learning cannot come back to their upright position of distinction from the world. This is the time when we should carefully study the models that God has given to us. When the brethren in Australia were establishing Avondale College, Ellen White gave them a solemn warning.

> I have been shown that in our educational work we are not to follow the methods that have been adopted in our older established schools. There is among us too much clinging to old customs, and because of this we are far behind where we should be in the development of the third angel's message. Because men could not comprehend the purpose of God in the plans laid before us for the education of workers, methods have been followed in some of our schools which have retarded rather than advanced the work of God.[5]

The reason that this school was not to pattern even after the Adventist schools already established in the United States was the fact that they had been established in many ways contrary to the divine instruction.

Another school, with which Sister White was closely associated, was Madison College. Avondale and Madison represented, at their foundation, the models by which present-day Adventist colleges should be operated. It is, therefore, imperative that all those who have a genuine interest in higher education, and in the re-establishment of the divine pattern in our schools, should study carefully these educational programs. Thus, at the post-secondary level, as well as at the elementary and the secondary level, the Lord is giving His people an opportunity to re-evaluate the direction of Adventist education. Upon what we do at this level depends the fulfillment of the gospel commission, and therefore the return of Jesus. So much is at stake that we cannot ignore the responsibility at hand.

1. White, *Testimonies for the Church,* Volume 6, page 137.
2. See Ibid., pages 211, 212.
3. Ibid., page 138.
4. White, *Fundamentals of Christian Education,* page 536.
5. White, *Counsels to Parents, Teachers, and Students,* page 533.

SECTION E

Issues in Contemporary Education

Chapter 21
Social Relations[1]

A strange neurosis has spread across Adventist North America. Large numbers of parents feel that if their child does not find a marriage partner, at least by the end of college, the chances of Christian marriage are remote. This belief has led many to see the finding of a spouse at college as a major, and to many the primary reason for attending a Christian college. Because the anxiety is even greater for girls, there are many more young ladies in Adventist colleges than young men, a fact which causes an obvious problem.

It should be stated that a Christian college can be a fine place to meet a life partner, as many can well testify.[2] But the emphasis upon dating and socializing at a Christian institution has frequently derailed the God-given mission of the institution. An objective view of the marriage scene indicates that, even within the church, divorce is at epidemic proportions. It is clear that preparation for marriage and the marriage relationship itself have been seriously injured by conformity to worldly influences. A careful study of divine counsel indicates that the present dating, in preparation for marriage, is not in accordance with heavenly principles, and no doubt has much to do with troubled marriages in the church. God's simple time-honored plan calls for young people to learn to know each other in a way that is not confused or complicated by emotional attachments reinforced by intimate physical relationships. In the freer, non-threatening environment of group relationships, character, temperament, and life direction can be discovered in a way that can more readily lead to prayerful, intelligent choices that are most likely to secure the future of a happy marriage.

During life, four major decisions with overriding significance are made:

1. The decision for Christ

2. Preparation for a life calling

3. The choice of a life partner

4. The decision to initiate a new life into the world.[3]

It is inevitably best if these decisions are made in the above order. Yet, frequently, they are made in the reverse order, causing social and emotional chaos and anguish. Even worse, it is rare, even in Christian families, if the above order is fully followed. The decision for Christ is an all-embracing one, affecting every other decision, great or small, in life. Tragic can be the consequences of making major decisions, such as the ones referred to above, before the commitment of our lives to Christ. Not only are our lives affected, but frequently those of many others. Many young people, caught in the valley of indecision, are urged to make other momentous decisions before this commitment is effectuated. The Christian parent and educator errs when such encouragement is made. Until the issues of eternity are settled, this decision must be the central focus of education.

Once the surrender of the life has been made, then the student has the divine resources to choose and prepare for a life calling. The truly converted youths will not yield to egocentric motivation, but will seek to discover the most effective way that he can witness God's love and call to others. It is self-evident that vocational choices that are made before Christian commitment may complicate later efforts by the Holy Spirit to woo the individual to Christ.

Perhaps there is no area where more premature decisions are made among Christians than in the area of marriage. Colin has spent many years in college teaching and administration, and has seen the sad results of precipitated relationships. This danger, together with the central purpose of preparation for God's work, is no doubt the reason that students are urged not to commence courtships while completing their education for Christian service.

> I do not wish to have you disappointed in regard to Battle Creek. The rules are strict there. No courting is allowed. The school

would be worth nothing to students were they to become en-
tangled in love affairs as you have been. Our college would soon
be demoralized.[4]

While at school, students should not allow their minds to become confused by thoughts of courtship. They are there to gain a
fitness to work for God, and this thought is ever to be upper-
most. Let all students take as broad a view as possible of their
obligations to God. Let them study earnestly how they can do
practical work for the Master during their student life.[5]

To the young men and young women who are being educated as
nurses and physicians I will say, Keep close to Jesus. By beholding
Him we become changed into His likeness. Remember that you
are not training for courtship or marriage, but for the marriage
of Christ.[6]

We have labored hard to keep in check everything in the school
like favoritism, attachments, and courting. We have told the students that we would not allow the first thread of this to be interwoven with their school work. On this point we were as firm as a
rock. I told them that they must dismiss all idea of forming attachments while at school. The young ladies must keep themselves to themselves, and the young gentlemen must do the same.[7]

There was a time, in most Adventist colleges up until the end of World
War II, when dating or courtship was not permitted on Adventist college
campuses; indeed, those planning for denominational service were rarely
permitted to marry before one year of successful ministry. No doubt some
will quickly argue that "times have changed," but, surely, the counsel of
the Lord has not changed. Others hasten to argue that children entered
college much younger, and that courtship was permitted for older, more
mature, and dedicated young people. No such counsel, however, can be
found in the Spirit of Prophecy. One statement often used to support this
concept is the following:

In all our dealings with students, age and character must be taken
into account. We cannot treat the young and old just alike. There
are circumstances under which men and women of sound experience and good standing may be granted some privileges not

given to the younger students. The age, the conditions, and the turn of the mind must be taken into consideration. We must be wisely considerate in all our work.[8]

It should be noted, however, that the quotation says nothing concerning courting, and this should be taken in context with what is stated about courtship.[9] Further, the continuance of the statement is important.

But we must not lessen our firmness and vigilance in dealing with students of all ages, nor our strictness in forbidding the unprofitable and unwise association of young and immature students.

In our schools in Battle Creek, Healdsburg, and Cooranbong, I have borne a straight testimony concerning these matters. There were those who thought the restraint too severe; but we told them plainly what could be and what could not be, showing them that our schools are established at great expense for a definite purpose, and that all which would hinder the accomplishment of this purpose must be put away.[10]

No doubt the concessions referred to by Ellen White were of a nature other than courting or dating. It must be remembered that she wrote in a time when our colleges had very strict rules in terms of male/female contact. Young men sat on one side of the chapel and of the church, and young women in assigned seats on the other side. There were restricted areas for young men and young women to walk, days and weekends for young men to leave campus, and for young women alternating. Cafeteria seating was assigned. The authors personally experienced these rules while students at Avondale College in 1950–51. And many of them were still enforced two decades later. In North America they tended to break down under the pressure of G.I.s returning from World War II, who claimed they were older, more mature, and had been deprived of female companionship for some time. It was probably to some of these earlier restrictions that Ellen White was referring, when she suggested that some additional privileges should be given to responsible students.

Some have wondered whether this counsel was given because college students were younger at that time. While it is true there were a few younger students, this was the exception not the rule. While they were students, the authors well-remember the young men's worships at

Avondale, presented by the late Pastor A. H. Piper, a man who lived about a year and a half in the home of Ellen White. He was about 22 when he entered Avondale College and, like many early students, was older than the average entrance age today, because there had been no other Adventist college, at that time, to attend. It is also noteworthy that the students did not graduate from academy level courses, but were fitted for denominational service.

In keeping step with the rapid decline in society's morality and pressure from worldly institutions, most Adventist schools and colleges have dramatically declined in the area of social relations. While it can be successfully argued that Adventist schools are still a far cry from some public schools, honesty demands that we acknowledge that we have fallen far away from the wise platform that God has given in respect to social relationships. Today one has to speak to the grandparents and, in some cases, the great-great-grandparents, to learn of what God's better plan was, and how it was implemented in our schools and colleges.

We can never be satisfied just to be better than the world. God has a principle of life for His children, in absolute contrast to the world. The results of early dating and strong emotional and physical ties are reaping a whirlwind of heartache in our church today. Blindly, we have argued that banquets provide a basis for learning social skills and how to relate properly to the opposite sex. The perceptive Christian educator sees rather the dangerous consequences of these immature relationships.

Almost every school has those who act as matchmakers, and who find delight in manipulating the young and the immature into relationships which are destined to produce anguish and uncertainty. Often this is fostered, even at the elementary school level. Yet large numbers of deans, especially girls' deans, report the unwholesome effects of banquet nights. Many deans stay up very late that night comforting the girls who have received no invitations. It might well be argued that this is life, but academy-aged children are far too immature to handle such pressure. They should have the freedom to grow up without such pressures inflicted upon them by unwise adults.

Is it any wonder that promiscuity is so rampant among even the children of church members? The popular girl cannot handle the adulation placed upon her, and often long before she has surrendered her life to Christ, she has yielded to compromising circumstances. The less popular girl who rarely receives an invitation is hardly better off. For when invited, she is under so much pressure to retain the attention of the boy in order to salvage some vestige of self-image among her peers, and often her superordinates also, that she permits almost free rein in the abuse of her body, if such pressure is applied by her escort.

The dating game is fraught with many hazards. To many young people, success or lack of it in "playing the game" is almost the sole determinant of self-image. Often adults, including parents, add to the stress. Almost completely lost sight of is the real basis of self-worth, nothing that humanity can achieve but the value which was placed upon each of us by God in the infinite Gift of His Son. Further, the dating game panders to the self-seeking motives of the youths. It is built upon finding one's own partner, and often getting as much as possible out of him or her. The conversation in the dormitories, after a banquet night, is positive proof to anyone who hears it, as to the negative, self-centered approach that is fostered.

Having extensively studied into Learning Theory, both authors wonder why many intelligent people fail to realize the dangers of dating, as a preparation for marriage. Having conducted weeks of prayer on academy campuses and having spoken with many youths who were troubled by sexual practices, both authors have inevitably encountered the issue of dating. Some boys, before the completion of high school, have dated so many girls that they have lost count. One day these same boys stand at the altar, vowing to "love, honor, and cherish until death do us part, and keep thee only unto myself as long as we both shall live."

But such young men for many years have habituated themselves to casting their affection on a variety of young women, and have learned the short-lived exhilaration of such activities. However sincere they may be when making their marriage vows, only the grace of God can keep these youths, in mind and action, true to their partners. If deep sensual activities and sexual relationships have taken place beforehand, especially with a number of different partners, it is well-nigh impossible for them to keep their marriage vows.

Is it any wonder that brides have confessed, "Even on our honeymoon, he began looking at other women." The seeds of marital disharmony and infidelity are firmly sown in the modern Western way of marriage preparation. Is it any wonder that God has an altogether different, a better plan for the preparation of His sons and daughters for marriage? This plan does not allow for young people to call out the affections of others, when it is not possible or wise for a lasting commitment to be made. Such a course results in irreparable damage to the youths. Rather, God's plan provides for the freedom of young people to mix in healthy group activities, where they can enjoy each other's company; getting to know each other in an environment, where they are liberated from the pressures of the dating game, where nobody is trying to link young men and women together in couples because they are seen talking together, and where they can give sanctified attention to their major responsibility of preparation for the great task of Spirit-filled ministry.

The wise young man and woman will be pressured into marriage by no one, not even their own parents. They will realize that marriage responsibilities are for mature people, who have carefully and prayerfully determined their readiness to explore this step. No doubt, in their church and school life, they have met other God-surrendered, seriously minded young people, who may share their goals and ministry commitment. From there, by counseling with godly adults, they will be led of Christ to form a lifelong commitment, where together their individual ministries will be enhanced.

For the young people committed to God's leading in this all-important step of life, there are a number of readiness factors that should be carefully considered.

1. **Spiritual Commitment**—Is Christ first and complete in our lives? Will our marriage enrich our ministries? Is the knowledge of God and the study of His truth paramount in our lives? Do we know how to share the great Advent truth with others?

2. **Educational Preparation**—Have we completed our education to the point where we are now ready for fuller service for God?

3. **Life Calling**—Do we have an understanding of the specific ministry into which the Lord is calling us? Are these callings compatible in a way that will not cause friction later?

4. **Social and Emotional Maturity**—Are we able to make wise, independent decisions based upon Christian principles? Is our self-image secure in Christ? Have we learned how to share rather than to be dependent upon getting, for security? Is our love built upon principle rather than emotion?

5. **Economic Readiness**—Are we able to handle money responsibly? Do we sense our stewardship obligations to God and our fellowman? Do we have sufficient agreement on the handling of the financial resources

of a home? Do we have sufficient income to provide for a life that will not bring discredit to the Lord? Are we free from major crippling debt?

6. **Agreement**—Do we share agreement on life's goals? Do we have harmony on family size and management? Do we have support in the relationship from our family and from wise spiritual counselors?

7. **Household Skills**—Do we have practical skills that support the needs of the home? Is the wife skilled in nutritious cooking, garment construction, gardening, and so on? Is the husband experienced in simple maintenance and gardening skills?

---

1. For a more detailed investigation of this topic, see *Family Crisis—God's Solution,* also by Drs. Standish.
2. Russell first met his wife while a student at Avondale College.
3. See chapter entitled, "The Education of Adolescents."
4. White, *Testimonies for the Church,* Volume 5, page 109.
5. White, *Counsels to Parents, Teachers, and Students,* page 100.
6. White, *Counsels on Health,* page 590.
7. White, *Manuscript Releases,* Volume 8, page 256.
8. White, *Counsels to Parents, Teachers, and Students,* page 101.
9. Ibid., page 100, quoted previously.
10. Ibid., page 101.

Chapter 22
Work Education

Work education has always been an integral part of God-centered education. In the Garden of Eden, our first parents were given a beautiful garden in which to develop their physical resources.

> And the LORD God planted a garden eastward in Eden; and there He put the man whom He had formed (Genesis 2:8).

After sin, work was an entirely different proposition for man; nevertheless, it was still to be a blessing.

> Thorns also and thistles shall it bring forth to thee; and thou shalt eat of the herb of the field; in the sweat of thy face shalt thou eat bread, till thou return unto the ground (Genesis 3:18, 19).

This work education, however, had deeper significance than the physical development of Adam and Eve.

> To Adam and Eve was committed the care of the garden. . . . Though rich in all that the Owner of the universe could supply, they were not to be idle. Useful occupation was appointed them as a blessing, to strengthen the body, to expand the mind, and to develop the character.[1]

It will be seen that work is not only essential to physical health and development but also to the development of the mind and the character.

In today's age, dominated by apartment living and almost unlimited labor-saving devices, this insight alone might give us some idea of the reason for the intellectual and moral weakness of the present age. While many see work as a burden, it was indeed given to be a blessing so that the character of man might be rounded and complete. As we have noted earlier[2] every Jewish child learned a trade, irrespective of his direction in life. Christ learned the trade of a carpenter.

> Jesus lived in a peasant's home, and faithfully and cheerfully acted His part in bearing the burdens of the household. . . . He learned a trade, and with His own hands worked in the carpenter's shop with Joseph. . . .

> As Jesus worked in childhood and youth, mind and body were developed. He did not use His physical powers recklessly, but in such a way as to keep them in health, that He might do the best work in every line. He was not willing to be defective, even in the handling of tools. He was perfect as a workman, as He was perfect in character. By His own example He taught that it is our duty to be industrious, that our work should be performed with exactness and thoroughness, and that such labor is honorable. The exercise that teaches the hands to be useful and trains the young to bear their share of life's burdens gives physical strength, and develops every faculty. All should find something to do that will be beneficial to themselves and helpful to others. God appointed work as a blessing, and only the diligent worker finds the true glory and joy of life. The approval of God rests with loving assurance upon children and youth who cheerfully take their part in the duties of the household, sharing the burdens of father and mother. Such children will go out from the home to be useful members of society. [3]

Likewise, the highly educated Paul was trained in a trade.

> Because he was of the same craft, he abode with [Aquila and Priscilla], and wrought: (for by their occupation they were tentmakers) (Acts 18:3).

Because there has been such a decided diminution of work opportunities for children in most homes, the development of work education in school becomes even more critical. Without this education the students cannot be given the balance that God has required of them. Many will be called to do special self-supporting work for God, and the acquisition of a trade and manual skills will allow them the greatest opportunity to support themselves and their families in this ministry. Even those who are being called to professional lines will benefit greatly from the ability to ply a skill, thus giving refreshment to the mind and the opportunity to have the fulfillment of well-accomplished tasks.

Work education provides, for the students, lifelong physical activity which will not militate against the service orientation of true Christian commitment; but, indeed, it will enhance the ministry of all. The development of careful skills not only is a challenge to the mind, but also facilitates in the development of moral attitudes, even to the simplest tasks of life. The satisfaction of a well-accomplished task is an altogether different satisfaction from that which is obtained in the victory on the sporting field. Indeed, it is not the heightened, transitory exhilaration of defeat of another individual or team, but it is the joy of seeing something well-accomplished which is of value and of purpose, and which in no wise depreciates the efforts of another.

Much modern-day counsel has been given concerning this much neglected form of education.

> In establishing our schools out of the cities, we shall give the students an opportunity to train the muscles to work as well as the brain to think. Students should be taught how to plant, how to gather the harvest, how to build, how to become acceptable missionary workers in practical lines. By their knowledge of useful industries they will often be enabled to break down prejudice; often they will be able to make themselves so useful that the truth will be recommended by the knowledge they possess.[4]

The authors well-remember the experience of a pastor that once served their church. Some years before, he had been located in a country town where he occasionally spent time with the local blacksmith. The pastor himself had been well-educated as a blacksmith in his younger days; and, on one occasion when the town blacksmith was seeking to determine how best to join two different metals together, the pastor was able to offer to him the best solution. This opening wedge ultimately led to the conversion of this man and his family. Many others can testify to the effectiveness of plying their trade in the witnessing of Christ's love to their fellowman. No education, which ignores the development of practical skills, can be authentic Christian education, for manual labor is integral to God-centered education.

> Useful manual labor is a part of the gospel plan. The Great Teacher, enshrouded in the pillar of cloud, gave directions to Israel that every youth should be taught some line of useful employment. Therefore it was the custom of the Jews, the wealthy as well as the poorer classes, to teach their sons and daughters some useful trade, so that, should adverse circumstances arise, they would not be dependent upon others, but would be able to provide for their own necessities. They might be instructed in literary lines, but they must also be trained to some craft. This was deemed an indispensable part of their education.

> Now, as in the days of Israel, every youth should be instructed in the duties of practical life. Each should acquire a knowledge of some branch of manual labor by which, if need be, he may obtain a livelihood. This is essential, not only as a safeguard against the vicissitudes of life, but from its bearing upon physical, mental, and moral development. [5]

Thus even those planning to enter a profession should be trained in some manual skill.

> The benefit of manual training is needed also by professional men. A man may have a brilliant mind; he may be quick to catch ideas; his knowledge and skills may secure for him admission to his chosen calling; yet he may still be far from possessing a fitness for its duties. An education derived chiefly from books leads to superficial thinking. Practical work encourages close observation and independent thought. Rightly performed, it tends to develop that practical wisdom which we call common sense. [6]

It is in the sphere of moral development, however, that practical education is most important.

> The essential lesson of contented industry in the necessary duties of life is yet to be learned by many of Christ's followers. It requires more grace, more stern discipline of character, to work for God in the capacity of mechanic, merchant, lawyer, or farmer, carrying the precepts of Christianity into the ordinary business

of life, than to labor as an acknowledged missionary in the open field. It requires a strong spiritual nerve to bring religion into the workshop and the business office, sanctifying the details of every-day life, and ordering every transaction according to the standard of God's word. But this is what the Lord requires.[7]

It was God's purpose to alleviate by toil the evil brought into the world by man's disobedience.... And though attended with anxiety, weariness, and pain, labor is still a source of happiness and development, and a safeguard against temptation. Its discipline places a check on self-indulgence, and promotes industry, purity, and firmness. Thus it becomes a part of God's great plan for our recovery from the Fall.[8]

It is for this reason that we are counseled that if any part of education is to be neglected, it should not be work education;' indeed, if a choice is to be made between academic and work education, the work is to be given priority. Ideally, there should be at least as much time every day given to work education as there is to the study of academics. This is not in any way to depreciate the study of books, but it is to place the priority upon that which will develop the skills and ministry of work; thus, the school day should be divided between an academic preparation and a work preparation. Some feel that this goal cannot be accomplished; but, wherever it has been attempted, it has been found that the students perform even better in their academic skills. Much time given over to the unprofitable development of skills in competitive sports is best devoted to learning valuable work ethics and education. As stated earlier, there was a time when practical education was greatly depreciated by many educational theorists, to the point that many referred to academic preparation as education and the learning of physical tasks as training. Even today there is still a tendency to rate much more highly the work of the mind than the work of the body. But such is not inconsistent with the counsel of God.

Work education is a requirement for the Christian school, and we have often been greatly negligent in it, thus depriving our children and youth of the unlimited value of the program. When children have a well-balanced work-study-outreach program, they have the basis for the development of the physical, mental, and spiritual facets of their lives, in a way that will maximize the claims of Christ upon their lives and service. Thus, work should not be simply an addendum to the curriculum. It

175

should be an integral part of the curriculum, in which the teachers, in an apprenticeship manner, work with and educate the children in their care. For this reason, our schools should provide adequate land so that agriculture and industries can be developed. These should not be industries that cause a burden to the financial operation of the school. They should be so well-planned and executed that they alleviate much of the crippling debt which now is afflicting so many of our schools. It is important that the children be trained in careful financial management. If they are going to use these skills later in their own self-supporting ministry, they need to know how to do so profitably, and in a manner which will support their ministry. With enthusiastic and capable management, these industries could so profit the finances of the school that major reductions could be made in the cost of student tuition. This would encourage many young people now being educated in public schools to return to a Christian environment.

In many instances, serious consideration should be given to the converting of large, expensive gymnasiums into work industries by which the students could profit in every way. There are some who have sought to operate a work-study-sports program. This is not according to God's plan; for, almost inevitably, the excitement and thrill of the sports will overshadow the work, depreciating it in the life and experience of the students. Sports are inimical to Christian growth and development, for they foster rivalry and egocentric goals. Work, on the other hand, provides cooperative ventures and worthwhile and valuable ends which are at the heart of Christian education.

1. White, *Education*, page 21.
2. See chapter entitled, "Physical Education."
3. White, *The Desire of Ages*, page 72.
4. White, *Counsels to Parents, Teachers, and Students*, pages 309, 310.
5. Ibid., page 307.
6. White, *Education*, page 220.
7. White, *Counsels to Parents, Teachers, and Students*, page 279.
8. Ibid., page 274.

Chapter 23
Recreational Education

For most people, their occupations are either primarily physical or sedentary in nature. For the first time in the history of the world, some countries have more white-collar than blue-collar workers. One of the primary purposes of recreation is to provide a balance for the individual's life. If one's occupation is primarily physical, it would logically follow that much recreational time should be spent in reading and the more intellectual pursuits. Conversely, for those whose occupation is sedentary, it is mandatory that considerable out-of-work time be spent in physically demanding activities.

The purpose of Christian recreation is to revitalize the individual for useful service rather than to provide unprofitable excitement. It is not an end in itself, but serves the broader purpose of revitalization. Ellen White puts it this way:

> There is a distinction between recreation and amusement. Recreation, when true to its name, re-creation, tends to strengthen and build up. Calling us aside from our Ordinary cares and occupations, it affords refreshment for mind and body, and thus enables us to return with new vigor to the earnest work of life. Amusement, on the other hand, is sought for the sake of pleasure and is often carried to excess; it absorbs the energies that are required for useful work and thus proves a hindrance to life's true success.[1]

It is especially important that children, who are in school, spend much of their time in energetic physical activities because of the sedentary nature of school room activity. Those schools which provide a strong work/

study program do much to balance the education of the child, but even this is rarely enough for the pent-up energies of youth. Thus we are counseled:

> Vigorous exercise the pupils must have. Few evils are more to be dreaded than indolence and aimlessness.[2]

But there are forms of physical activity which are unsuitable for, and counterproductive to, Christian growth. Activities which addictively absorb the time to the extent that they begin to draw students away from productive work, from service activities, and love for God, can have no rightful place in Christian education. Thus, competitive games, especially those which have a counterpart in professional sports, prove counterproductive.

> They stimulate the love of pleasure and excitement, thus fostering a distaste for useful labor, a disposition to shun practical duties and responsibilities. They tend to destroy a relish for life's sober realities and its tranquil enjoyments. Thus the door is opened to dissipation and lawlessness, with their terrible results.[3]

The Christian parent and teacher also avoids those activities which tend toward lightness and frivolity. Some wrongly conclude that such activities are innocent fun. But they are far from innocent.

> As ordinarily conducted, parties of pleasure also are a hindrance to real growth, either of mind or of character. Frivolous associations, habits of extravagance, of pleasure seeking, and too often of dissipation, are formed, that shape the whole life for evil. In place of such amusements, parents and teachers can do much to supply diversions wholesome and life-giving.[4]

The question arises as to what are the wholesome and lifegiving activities that are available to the parent and teacher. An important starting point was explored by a one-time General Conference education director, W. E. Howell.

> The natural child in a natural environment finds natural delight in imitating what he sees his elders do. Natural play is essentially an imitation of work. The little girl likes to make mud pies, to play housekeeping, to teach school. The little boy likes to build a

house with his blocks, to tie a cord to his sister's arms and drive her about like a horse, to run his toy train. Unless influenced by the artificial on the part of his elders or companions, natural children are satisfied by these natural imitations of work, until as they grow up these imitations merge into real work.[5]

Howell clearly contrasts this with that recreation which is counterproductive to Christian growth and development.

But there is another kind of thing the world calls play, namely, the game. Though often used loosely, a game proper is a contest. The spirit of it is the spirit of competition, of beating the other fellow—either by surprising him in exploit, or by attaining the ultimate of putting him out of action. It exalts the victor, and humiliates the loser. While natural play is an imitation of work, this artificial play represented in the game is an imitation of fight, an imitation of war. The spirit of natural play is the spirit of work. The spirit of the game is the spirit of war.[6]

After a very shaky start, much progress was made in our schools and colleges in the early decades of this century. Yet, frequently, corrections had to be made. Howell quotes two such examples, one made by the Education Department of the Pacific Union and the other by Walla Walla College.

In view of the constant menace threatening our educational work by games and amusements: We recommend, That the faculty and board of each school in the Pacific Union Conference make a careful survey of its past customs with respect to games and amusements; and that in the future we undertake to put into practice the standards set before us in the Bible and the Spirit of Prophecy, to the effect that practical missionary work, useful manual labor, and other Christian recreational methods be substituted for games and amusements.[7]

Some have argued that, in today's age, it would be misunderstood if we did not allow some sports in our schools; indeed, it is regarded as fanatical by some to argue against sports. But it can hardly be designated fanatical if it is God's plan. A number of counsels clearly make this point.

> To spend money, which is so hard to obtain, on materials with which to play tennis and cricket is not in harmony with the testimonies which have been given to our school in Battle Creek . . .

> It has been understood all through our ranks that these games are not the proper education to be given in any of our schools.[8]

> The time is altogether too full of tokens of the coming conflict to be educating the youth in fun and games. It pains my heart to read letters where these exercises are spoken about, and where they write such expressions as "Oh, we had so much fun" and such expressions.[9]

Another area of recreation needs to be addressed, the area of recreation which is mostly intellectual in nature. This may be a legitimate form of recreation, if wisely chosen. However, many of the table games, such as chess and checkers, have the same element of rivalry that other more physical sports have.

> There are amusements, such as dancing, card playing, chess, checkers, etc., which we cannot approve, because Heaven condemns them. These amusements open the door for great evil. They are not beneficial in their tendency, but have an exciting influence, producing in some minds a passion for those plays which lead to gambling and dissipation.[10]

Reading plays a vital role in recreation, as well as education. The authors were blessed by parents who gave only missionary and nature books to them. It could have helped provide the motivation that led both of us to mission service. Under no circumstances are imaginary and make-believe materials to be considered as suitable for the Christian child. With great care, it is possible to develop such a love for the Word of God that this will be considered a joy to read, even by pre-adolescent children.

In an age of shortened work weeks and less work around the home, the attention given to recreational activity which will further the Christian goals of the home and school is critical. The authors both excelled in sports in their youth, and well-know its danger to spiritual growth. Even today, they find the enticement of sports one of their greatest spiritual battles.

1. White, *Education,* page 207.
2. Ibid., pages 218.
3. Ibid, page 210, 211.
4. Ibid., page 211.
5. "Working to the Pattern in Christian Education," *Review and Herald,* March 25, 1926.
6. Ibid.
7. Ibid., September 1925.
8. White, *Manuscript Releases,* Volume 8, page 74.
9. White, Letter 46, 1893.
10. White, *Counsels to Parents, Teachers, and Students,* page 346.

Chapter 24
Outreach Education

The third aim of Christian education,[1] presented in this book, is the education of our children and youth in service for God and man. The converted person cries out for the reinforcement of his response to his newfound faith. Physiologically, his body is ready for action. The love response to his newfound faith leads to the motivation reaction of the sympathetic nervous system. If we challenge our youth to surrender, they are left in great peril if they are not also given the privilege of reinforcing that commitment in sharing with others.

The Scriptures are replete with examples of this fact. When Christ called Peter and Andrew, he provided a call to service.

> As He walked by the sea of Galilee, He saw Simon and Andrew his brother casting a net into the sea: for they were fishers. And Jesus said unto them, Come ye after Me, and I will make you to become fishers of men (Mark 1:16, 17).

Long before the disciples understood the fullness of the gospel they were, nevertheless, sent out to share what they did know.

> He called His twelve disciples together, and gave them power and authority over all devils, and to cure diseases. And He sent them to preach the kingdom of God, and to heal the sick. And He said unto them, Take nothing for your journey, neither staves, nor scrip, neither bread, neither money; neither have two coats apiece. And whatsoever house ye enter into, there abide, and thence depart. And whosoever will not receive you, when ye go out of that city, shake off the very dust from your feet for a testimony against

them. And they departed, and went through the towns, preaching the gospel, and healing every where (Luke 9:1–6).

The apostle Paul, after his Damascus-road conversion, reinforced his faith by witness, before the Lord led him to Arabia for further divine education.

> Barnabus took him, and brought him to the apostles, and declared unto them how he had seen the Lord in the way, and that He had spoken to him, and how he had preached boldly at Damascus in the name of Jesus. And he was with them coming in and going out at Jerusalem. And he spake boldly in the name of the Lord Jesus (Acts 9:27–29).

The fact that so many young people once were challenged by the love and power of God, but now are captive to the world, can surely be traced, in a large measure, to our failure to provide opportunities for them to witness their faith. Sadly, after a most challenging Sabbath, we have often provided the most suspect entertainment at night, feebly claiming the youth need the opportunity to "let their hair down." Indeed, the Spirit of God has been quenched, and the resulting conduct frequently leads to a greater unlikelihood of a subsequent response to the Spirit's call.

Some years ago an Australian university professor, representing a large student Christian society, addressed a gathering of students. After having denied the person of God, and having spent much time in debunking the Scriptures, the professor was confronted by a student who declared that, as an atheist, he could agree almost entirely with what had been said by the professor.

The professor was pleased that his discussion had been "relevant," even to an atheist. Yet even after the assembly, the student remained confused and disillusioned, apparently reinforced in the conviction of his no-God concept.

"Relevancy" has become the watchcry of modern Christendom. The very obvious eroding of the Christian impact upon the world has led church leaders to look for new ways to entice the masses back to the empty pews; thus, there has been a proliferation of views expressed and methods employed by church leaders, aimed to lift Christianity from its Victorian image. The most common appeal has been to the youth. Frantic attempts have been made to "get with" the inquisitive, independent, worldly-wise youth who are questioning the values in adult society.

Youth is an age of great challenges, of emerging ideals, of almost indefatigable energies, and of strengthening purposes. There is a willfulness, an independence, that belies the immaturity and uncertainty, and seeks to find values and goals worthy of achievement and worthy of life. It may be argued that to spark the vision of youth is to light an eternal flame. But today we see a worldwide dissipation of the energies of youth toward transient goals and unproductive activities.

The world that once promised peace has produced a sickening parade of wars, revolts, uprisings, rebellions, and chaos on an international scale. This is the world that's forced upon young people in this generation. They didn't choose it, they didn't make it, but they inherited it. Today they are revolting against what we who are older have given them.

In previous times it has been the peasant, the poor, the oppressed, the unemployed, who have revolted; but, today the seeds of revolt are fired in the breasts of the affluent, the intellectual, and the educated. No longer is the mature man at the end of his tether; it is youth, in all their emerging passions, who are decimating the social foundations of the second half of the twentieth century.

Establishment, institution, and authority are often despised. There is a certainty of what is not wanted, but no assurance of what is desired. Gone are the days when youth passively accepted what they were told, the parental style of life, the social structure into which they were born, of the values of existing society. The universities of the world have witnessed the terror of their youth in rebellion. Social values are fragmenting, the immutables are now the mores, the certainties the doubtfuls, the truths the questionables.

It is with the backdrop of this confusion that church leaders are frantically looking for revolutionary approaches to stem the tide, and re-establish Christianity in the community.

Unfortunately, the drive for relevancy has led many churchmen into the cul-de-sac of worldly entertainment and amusements, the dance hall, the jukeboxes, the coffee lounge, the cabaret. Even worse, almost every known sin has been declared to be sin no longer—from premarital sex and homosexuality to the blasphemous use of the name of God. There is a frenzied attempt to have youth identify themselves with the church, but no real burden to have them identify with the cross of Calvary. Worldly conformity is accepted and often encouraged, while the transforming power of the Holy Spirit is neither invited nor understood. Relevance has been the excuse to parade a social philosophy, rather than to uphold a spiritual destiny.

The Seventh-day Adventist Church faces the same burdening problems, as do other churches, in the challenges of its youth. Only the sense of a great mission and the eternal heritage of our youth can prevent us from stumbling into the same pitfalls as others have in the work for their youth.

Already the danger signs are present. There has been a tendency to increase activity for the youth rather than to institute a constant search for the fuller Christian development. In fact, on occasions, we have attempted to entertain our young people into the church; and, in so doing, we have unbelievably followed the same pathway as other church communities. We have seen films that God will not bless screened for entertainment; we have seen variety programs that have been a decided hindrance to the fuller understanding of the way of righteousness; we have witnessed sporting programs and intense competition that bespeak how little we recognize the task that is ours in training the youth for service. We have often given the husk and not the grain; and, tragically, our colleges have sometimes been in the forefront, fostering the pseudo-Christian approach.

Some years ago an Australian Olympic gold medalist swimmer was interviewed concerning his training program. He discussed the various exercises and calisthenic training that he undertook in his arduous preparation, and concluded with a significant comment, "But my main training is in the pool. I do at least five hours training there a day." All the exercises this young man did could never make him a champion swimmer. They were helpful, but they were supplementary to the basic training in the pool. So it is with the training of our young people. If we really want to make Christians of them, the basic training must be in the pool of Christian commitment and service. There will be an important place for well-chosen recreation and social activity, but these activities will, in themselves, never make a Christian; they will always be the supplementary training.

Many young people never become Christians because no one has ever shown them how, they have been unable to find the way. Today we face the tragedy of a majority of young people who have no idea of how to take hold of Christ. There is a tremendous challenge to the leaders of our young people, to offer to them the greatest relevancy that Christianity can offer—that of translating the principles of Christ into the very fabric of their lives.

Some time ago, Colin was invited to be chairman of a panel discussion with six youth, ranging from 14 to 18 years of age. All came from undivided Seventh-day Adventist homes; and all had, or were having, the opportunity of a Christian education; yet each confessed that he had never helped another to know Christ. Almost in desperation they said that they did not know how, but they wanted to know. The next morning a delegation came to say that a group of the young people had met together, and had decided to hold meetings for the purpose of learning how to become Christian workers.

How challenging this is to our parents, our Sabbath School teachers, our church school teachers, and our ministry! Many young people crave the opportunity to live and work for Christ. Surely this desire is the essence of relevancy. Relevancy is not taking Christianity to the level of wayward youth, but helping youth to understand how they may be transformed into the image of Christ. There is no greater relevance than to love our youth so much that we lead them to Christ, and help them to discover how to live and work for Him.

Authentic Christian education, from the home through the school system, must provide, as an integral part of the curriculum, effective, fulfilling service. The authors remember their opportunity as lads of going with their father on missionary service. The home is to be a missionary training ground. The school, as an education for service, is just as important. It will prove a witness to the world.

> The most important work of our educational institutions at this time is to set before the world an example that will honor God.[2]

It will witness through staff and students to the local community.

> When properly conducted, church schools will be the means of lifting the standard of truth in the places where they are established; for children who are receiving a Christian education will be witnesses for Christ.[3]

The churches should unite with schools in this work.

> There should be men and women who are qualified to work in the churches and to train our young people for special lines of work, that souls may be brought to see Jesus. The schools established by us should have in view this object, and not be after the order of the denominational schools established by other churches, or after the order of worldly seminaries and colleges.[4]

So effective should this preparation be, that youth who are completing high school or academy should be ready for such service.

> Intermediate [academy] schools are highly essential. In these schools thorough work is to be done; for many students will go forth from them directly into the great harvest field.[5]

The Christian school cannot be eclectic in this matter. Such education cannot be optional, for all students are to be provided the opportunity and privilege of such service.

> All who shall be educated in our schools, are to be trained to be workers.[6]

We have been counseled that the last possible avenue of witness will be medical missionary work; therefore, this avenue of education must be an essential part of the curriculum. The present interest, of secular society in health, emphasizes the importance of education in this ministry.

> I wish to tell you that soon there will be no work done in ministerial lines but medical missionary work. The work of a minister is to minister. Our ministers are to work on the gospel plan of ministering. . . .

> You will never be ministers after the gospel order till you show a decided interest in medical missionary work, the gospel of healing and blessing and strengthening.[7]

The experience of both authors is that a vast mission field is available through the medical missionary work. It is our conviction that the school that does not give high priority to outreach education in its community is not an authentic Christian school. The substitution of entertainment for service substitutes the egocentric activity for selfless service. Probably nothing is more responsible for the emotional, social, and spiritual ills of our youth than this one single factor.

1. See chapter entitled, "Foolishness and Wisdom."
2. White, *Counsels to Parents, Teachers, and Students,* page 57.
3. Ibid., page 176.
4. White, *Fundamentals of Christian Education,* page 231.
5. White, *Counsels to Parents, Teachers, and Students,* page 203.
6. White, *The Kress Collection,* page 67.
7. White, *Counsels on Health,* page 533.

Chapter 25
Dress Education

One of the most sensitive areas to address in education, and yet a very important one, is the area of dress. Personal appearance is perhaps the first impact that is made upon new acquaintances. The Christian has a very special reason to dress in a manner which will be most productive in gaining the respect of his fellow human beings. He is not to dress for personal glory nor to attract others to himself, but in such way as will complement his God-given character and attract men and women to the Lord.

> A person's character is judged by his style of dress. A refined taste, a cultivated mind, will be revealed in the choice of simple and appropriate attire.[1]

While Paul's counsel is specifically addressed to women, the principles are just as appropriate to men.

> In like manner also, that women adorn themselves in modest apparel, with shamefacedness, and sobriety; not with braided hair, or gold, or pearls, or costly array (1 Timothy 2:9).

Some will strongly argue that dress is an individual matter, and appropriateness of dress should not be a basis of Christian concern. Inspiration does not agree.

> No education can be complete that does not teach right principles in regard to dress. Without such teaching, the work of education is too often retarded and perverted. Love of dress, and

devotion to fashion, are among the teacher's most formidable rivals and most effective hindrances.[2]

Obedience to fashion is pervading our Seventh-day Adventist churches and is doing more than any other power to separate our people from God. I have been shown that our church rules are very deficient. All exhibitions of pride in dress, which is forbidden in the word of God, should be sufficient reason for church discipline.[3]

For the Christian a number of important principles will be carefully evaluated in terms of the choice of dress.

1. Influence—Above all, our Christian influence will override the style of dress that we use. That which will represent our Lord and Saviour, in an effective and appropriate way, will always be chosen.

In the name of my Master I appeal to the young men and women who claim to be sons and daughters of God, to obey the Word of God. I appeal to teachers in our schools to set a right example to those with whom they are associated. Those who would be qualified to mold the character of youth, must be learners in the school of Christ, that they may be meek and lowly of heart, as was the divine Pattern. In dress, in deportment, in all their ways, they should exemplify the Christian character, revealing the fact that they are under wise disciplinary rules of the great Teacher.[4]

The words of Scripture in regard to dress should be carefully considered. We need to understand that which the Lord of heaven appreciates in even the dressing of the body. All who are in earnest in seeking for the grace of Christ will heed the precious words of instruction inspired by God. Even the style of the apparel will express the truth of the gospel.[5]

2. Appropriateness—It is axiomatic that dress in one situation will be inappropriate in another. When we are representing Christ in special ministry, we should dress with the appropriateness of one representing the Lord in that activity; nevertheless, in the common pursuits of life, in our everyday activities, we will dress in a manner befitting our needs. This does not mean that modesty and health will not still be carefully preserved, but it does mean that clothes which are suitably constructed will be worn for the activity.

3. Economy—Economy does not mean that we will necessarily wear clothes of the cheapest construction; indeed, frequently, more expensive clothing will be worn, because, in the long term, it will be a better value.

> Our clothing, while modest and simple, should be of good quality, of becoming colors, and suited for service. It should be chosen for durability rather than display.[6]

4. Health—This is a most critical issue, especially in climates where the temperature range is great. Often fashion dictates most unhealthful patterns, but the Christian must not be enslaved by worldly customs which are transitory and inconsistent, in most cases, with the principles of God.

> [Our clothing] should provide warm and proper protection. The wise woman described in Proverbs "is not afraid of the snow for her household: for all her household are clothed with double garments" (Proverbs 31:21, margin).

> Our dress should be cleanly. Uncleanliness in dress is unhealthful, and thus defiling to the body and to the soul.[7]

5. Modesty—Perhaps no area is more closely associated with our Christian character than modesty. This goes beyond simplicity to include the area of bodily accentuation. So much modern dress is meant to accentuate the physical and draw attention to the sexuality of the individual. Much dress, both male and female, is of such a character that attention is focused upon the externals, making it almost impossible to look for the deeper and fuller inner beauty of character.

Perhaps no area of dress has been so clearly perverted today as the preservation of the distinctive roles of men and women. This distinction is very clearly enjoined in Scripture.

> The woman shall not wear that which pertaineth unto a man, neither shall a man put on a woman's garment: for all that do so are abomination unto the LORD thy God (Deuteronomy 22:5).

Some have felt that this text has exclusive designation to homosexual or lesbian cross-sex dressing or to men masquerading as women and women as men. But this is not so in the light of its more modern usage by Ellen White. In the 1860s America was embroiled in the women's rights controversy, in a situation paralleling the women's liberation movement

today. As now, dress had become an important insignia of this movement, with many women somehow feeling that equality means sameness.
While all Christians uphold the equality of men and women, they cannot, in the light of God-given counsel, equate this with sameness. Perhaps the real principle is equal but different. As in the 1860s, so now,
many women have militantly sought to dress like men, believing that
somehow this symbolizes equality. These, in turn, have infiltrated the fashion houses to the point that today many of the garments that are worn by
women, even by some who have no ties with the women's liberation movement, are identical with those of men. This practice is not at all in accordance with the principles of the gospel. True Christian men and women
seek to retain the distinctive identity with which men and women have
been created.

> I saw that God's order had been reversed, and His special direc-
> tions disregarded, by those who adopt the American costume
> [dress somewhat similar to a very conservative pants suit with a
> uniform-like top]. I was referred to Deuteronomy 22:5. . . . God
> would not have His people adopt the so-called reform dress. It is
> immodest apparel, wholly unfitted for the modest, humble fol-
> lowers of Christ.

> There is an increasing tendency to have women in their dress
> and appearance as near like the other sex as possible, and to fash-
> ion their dress very much like that of men, but God pronounces
> it abomination. [8]

It might be appropriate here to indicate God's attitude toward the
women's rights movement, which Ellen White has appropriately linked
with men's dress.

> Those who feel called out to join the movement in favor of
> woman's rights and the so-called dress reform might as well sever
> all connection with the third angel's message. The spirit which
> attends the one cannot be in harmony with the other. The Scrip-
> tures are plain upon the relations and rights of men and women. [9]

In the light of the clearest counsel that God can give, and in view of
Western culture, it cannot be appropriate for women to dress in pants
any more than it would be appropriate for a man to dress in dresses. It is
important to note that even secular observers have come to similar con-

clusions. A number of surveys have indicated that there is nothing more sexually provocative than tight pants on a woman. Further evidence has also indicated that whenever women's clothing becomes similar to that of men, the level of sexual promiscuity and sexual abuse of women significantly increases. There is an unconscious tendency for men to lose some of the respect and reserve that they should possess for members of the opposite sex; and, in so doing, the floodgate is opened to immorality.

> Chaste simplicity in dress, when united with modesty of demeanor, will go far toward surrounding a young woman with that atmosphere of sacred reserve which will be to her a shield from a thousand perils.[10]

Few areas need more urgent teaching in our church today than dress reform. This reform must not be presented from a legalistic viewpoint nor from a judgmental perspective; but, because of the rapid decline in standards and appropriateness of dress, the Christian needs to realize the total difference that he must present in his witness and representation of Christ. Some have argued that if we are going to have influence with those who dress according to modern standards, we must dress like them. But there is no evidence to support this argument. Indeed, the worldling recognizes that there should be a marked distinction between the Christian and himself.

Of particular significance should be the attention we give to the way we dress when we come into the house of the Lord. Increasing casualness and carelessness are marking the dress of God's people. It is interesting to note that in many non-Christian religions such dress is not tolerated.[11]

> I am often pained as I enter the house where God is worshiped, to see the untidy dress of both men and women. If the heart and character were indicated by the outward apparel, then certainly nothing could be heavenly about them. They have no true idea of the order, the neatness, and the refined deportment that God requires of all who come into His presence to worship Him. What impressions do these things give to unbelievers and to the youth, who are keen to discern and to draw their conclusions?[12]

At the time Ellen White was writing, there was a major problem in adornment and extravagance of dress; today, while this is still a problem with some, an even greater problem seems to be in dressing in an untidy and inappropriate manner. Both untidiness and elaborateness dishonor God, who is calling us back to the simple, representative dress of the Christian.

> The very class that have been presented before me as imitating the fashions of the world have been very slow, and the last, to be affected or reformed. Another class who lacked taste and order in dress have taken advantage of what I have written and have gone to the opposite extreme; considering that they were free from pride, they have looked upon those who dress neatly and orderly as being proud. Oddity and carelessness in dress have been considered a special virtue by some. Such take a course which destroys their influence over unbelievers. They disgust those whom they might benefit.

> While the visions have reproved pride and imitating the fashions of the world, they have also reproved those who were careless in regard to their apparel and lacked cleanliness of person and dress.[13]

A very important principle to be considered is that we tend to act the way that we dress. This fact has specific implication for our Sabbath dress. Many who may dress appropriately for the Sabbath services seem to show indecent haste to get into the most casual and inappropriate dress as soon as they return to their homes. This practice has a tendency to open a floodgate of temptation, to forget the sacredness and the beauty of the Sabbath hours. The counsel that has been given does not apply only to the house of worship.

> Especially have I been shown that those who profess present truth should have a special care to appear before God upon the Sabbath in a manner which would show that we respect the Creator who has sanctified and placed special honors upon that day. All who have any regard for the Sabbath should be cleanly in person, neat and orderly in dress; for they are to appear before the jealous God, who is offended at uncleanness and disorder, and who marks every token of disrespect.[14]

God has given special counsel to those who have a special ministry in His church.

There should be no carelessness in dress. For Christ's sake, whose witnesses we are, we should seek to make the best of our appearance. In the tabernacle service, God specified every detail concerning the garments of those who ministered before Him. Thus we are taught that He has a preference in regard to the dress of those who serve Him. Very specific were the directions given in regard to Aaron's robes, for his dress was symbolic. So the dress of Christ's followers should be symbolic. In all things we are to be representatives of Him. Our appearance in every respect should be characterized by neatness, modesty, and purity. But the word of God gives no sanction to the making of changes in apparel merely for the sake of fashion, that we may appear like the world. Christians are not to decorate the person with costly array or expensive ornaments.[15]

When we consider the amount of carelessness and apostasy in the church, we must not overlook the influence of dress upon this trend.

I have been shown that the main cause of your backsliding is your love of dress. This leads to the neglect of grave responsibilities, and you find yourselves with scarcely a spark of the love of God in your hearts. Without delay, renounce the cause of your backsliding, because it is sin against your own soul and against God. Be not hardened by the deceitfulness of sin. Fashion is deteriorating the intellect and eating out the spirituality of our people. Obedience to fashion is pervading our Seventh-day Adventist churches, and is doing more than any other power to separate our people from God.[16]

A pure and holy God is calling His people back to a fit and appropriate representation of Him. As the character of Jesus is perfectly reproduced in His people, this character will also be exemplified in dress which will honor the God whom they represent. Perhaps no one puts it more clearly than Peter, as he applies the principles which are of significance to both men and women.

Whose adorning let it not be that outward adorning of plaiting the hair, and of wearing of gold, or of putting on of apparel; but let it be the hidden man of the heart, in that which is not cor-

ruptible, even the ornament of a meek and quiet spirit, which is
in the sight of God of great price (1 Peter 3:3, 4).

1. White, *Education,* page 248.
2. Ibid., page 246.
3. White, *Testimonies for the Church,* Volume 4, page 647.
4. White, *Fundamentals of Christian Education,* page 191.
5. White, *Testimonies for the Church,* Volume 6, page 96.
6. White, *Ministry of Healing,* page 288.
7. Ibid.
8. White, *Testimonies for the Church,* Volume 1, page 457.
9. Ibid.
10. White, *Education,* page 248.
11. Russell has seen the shock of Buddhist visitors to Seventh-day Adventist churches, where Western visitors have entered the church in shorts, shirts, and scuffs.
12. White, *Testimonies for the Church,* Volume 5, page 498.
13. Ibid., Volume 1, page 275.
14. Ibid.
15. Ibid., Volume 6, page 96.
16. Ibid., Volume 4, page 647.

Chapter 26
What About Accreditation?

Accreditation and state-approval processes are of comparatively recent origin. Therefore, we do not find unequivocal counsel upon this topic. Perhaps the closest counsel concerning the issue is given in respect to the development of the medical school at the College of Medical Evangelism (now Loma Linda University). When the question of meeting state standards arose, Ellen White had this to say:

> The medical school at Loma Linda is to be of the highest order, because those who are in that school have the privilege of maintaining a living connection with the wisest of all physicians, from whom there is communicated knowledge of a superior order. And for the special preparation of those of our youth who have clear convictions of their duty to obtain a medical education that will enable them to pass the examinations required by law of all who practice as regularly qualified physicians, we are to supply whatever may be required, so that these youth need not be compelled to go to medical schools conducted by men not of our faith.[1]

> What He has promised, He will do, and inasmuch as there are legal requirements making it necessary that medical students shall take a certain preparatory course of study, our colleges should arrange to carry their students to the point of literary and scientific training that is necessary.[2]

However, these statements are to be understood in the very deliberate context of what Ellen White has given.

I am instructed to say that in our education work there is to be no compromise in order to meet the world's standards. God's commandment-keeping people are not to unite with the world to carry various lines of work according to worldly plans and worldly wisdom.

Our people are now being tested as to whether they will obtain their wisdom from the greatest Teacher the world ever knew, or seek to the god of Ekron. Let us determine that we shall not be tied by so much as a thread to the educational policies of those who do not discern the voice of God, and who will not hearken to His commandments.[3]

Some questions have been asked me regarding our relation to the laws governing medical practitioners. We need to move understandingly, for the enemy would be pleased to hedge up our work so that our physicians would have only a limited influence. Some men do not act in the fear of God, and they may seek to bring us into trouble by placing on our necks yokes that we could not consent to bear. We cannot submit to regulations if the sacrifice of principles is involved; for this would imperil the soul's salvation.

But whenever we can comply with the law of the land without putting ourselves in a false position, we should do so. Wise laws have been framed in order to safeguard the people against the imposition of unqualified physicians. These laws we should respect, for we are ourselves by them protected from presumptuous pretenders.[4]

There is constant danger among our people that those who engage in labor in our schools and sanitariums will entertain the idea that they must get in line with the world, study the things which the world studies, and become familiar with the things that the world becomes familiar with. This is one of the greatest mistakes that could be made. We shall make grave mistakes unless we give special attention to the searching of the word.[5]

The issue of accreditation reached an unprecedented intensity at the beginning of the 1930s. It was during the 1931 Autumn [Annual] Council in Omaha, Nebraska, that the issue of accreditation of our colleges and schools was given consideration. The decision was to enter upon an accrediting program for our institutions. At this council, Elder C. H. Watson, then president of the General Conference, presided. There was an attempt to move into it in a very careful way. Later Elder W. H. Branson, then vice-president of the General Conference, and later General Conference president, put it this way:

> It was described at that time by one of our leading workers as being a war measure. It was stated in the action itself that it was an emergency measure. The reason for the emergency seemed to be the fact that we were facing a situation, as we understood it, that would make it all but impossible to go on with certain lines of training unless our schools were accredited. That is true of the medical work. They stated that it would be impossible for the college to receive students from junior and senior colleges unless these colleges were accredited with regional accrediting associations.

> It was also stated that we had reached a time when teacher training could not be carried on in an unaccredited school in a satisfactory way. The requirements were such as to make necessary, they said, the accrediting of schools for the training of our teachers.

> Then there were also a number of us that, in the training of nurses, thought it was necessary in some places that the prenursing should be given in accredited schools. So we felt under great pressure as, in council, we studied this question four years ago and arrived at a conclusion I have already stated.[6]

Elder Branson further described certain safeguards that were voted:

> Wherewith, we know full-well from observation and repeated warnings from the Spirit of Prophecy that by sending our teachers to the universities of the world for advanced degrees, we are exposing them to great dangers, as is evidenced by the number of our men who have already in this way lost their hold upon God, and realizing that there is great danger to our system of Christian education through the molding influence of these worldly schools on our teachers.

We recommend that, in the selection of teachers to attend the universities, only persons of outstanding Christian experience and who have been successful in Christian work should be chosen; that persons whose faith in the Bible and Spirit of Prophecy is well-grounded; and who realize that, in attending the university, they are being exposed to subtle and almost unconscious infidelity—persons who believe with all their hearts in the superiority of Christian education.[7]

However, later in his address, Elder Branson had to declare:

We believe, Brother Chairman, as a result of our study of this situation, that the safeguards that we tried to throw around the policy of accrediting four years ago when we entered upon this course have very largely broken down. Therefore we entered upon a course that we did not plan on, and we know that things have gone further than was anticipated. We are facing dangers and perils in this matter of accrediting our colleges that were little dreamed of at the time when this action was taken four years ago. For instead of a few teachers being selected carefully by college boards as was recommended, teachers who would represent outstanding Christian experience, and who have been successful in their Christian work, whose fidelity to the Bible and testimonies is unquestioned, we have found that a large class of very young and immature people have been finding their way into the universities believing that as a highway to appointment in our institutional work. They have not waited to gain these years of Christian experience—experience that comes through years of Christian service. They have not waited to be chosen by some board that would carefully weigh the question of whether or not this or that individual should go to the university.[8]

He later warned:

We believe that, as a result of what has taken place, the wrong emphasis has been placed on certain things in our work. We believe undue emphasis is being placed upon the idea of securing degrees from worldly institutions rather than training our youth for spiritual service in the cause of God. I suppose many of us could honestly testify that we have been hearing more during the past four years about degrees and accreditation and universities than we have heard in our lifetimes.[9]

Finally, Elder Branson concluded:

> We believe that we should endeavor to change the emphasis that has been placed on worldly standards and degrees; that we should begin to turn the emphasis in our educational work upon training young men and women to go out and preach the message with power, young women to go out as Bible workers and also teach this message with power; and to train young men and women to go to the mission fields in the world with strong abiding faith in God and this message, without having their faith lessened or in any way minimized by contact with worldly schools and organizations that do not believe in God and this message. We should train them in our own schools and ignore the standards of the world to a large degree, to the degree that these standards modify the standards of Seventh-day Adventists.[10]

Unfortunately the plea of Elder Branson did not fall upon receptive ears. Once we had moved towards the issue of accreditation, there seemed to be no turning back. While the cry had once been that we can always reverse the situation; indeed, in reality, that has not been the case. Hardly any of our schools down through the years have made any attempt to reverse the situation, irrespective of where it has led them.

Branson was far from being a lone voice on this accreditation issue. A number of other prominent leaders also expressed their viewpoints. An example of this came in an article by H. J. Klooster:

> There are among our people those who look upon the present program of accrediting our schools with apprehension and concern. Their concern for the outcome of our present program is not without just cause. Through the years some of our most brilliant young men who have attended various universities and institutions of higher learning have lost their way in a morass of philosophic speculation. In some instances the appeal of larger financial compensation than our schools could afford to pay has drawn our capable young educators, through the universities, into the service of the world, resulting not only in a large loss of talent

to our own work, but usually in spiritual atrophy of the individuals.[11]

It is most commonly argued that regional accrediting organizations in the United States at no time call for compromise of principle or Christian standards; and that they evaluate consistently, only with the philosophy of the institution. Yet the honest evaluator, of what has taken place under accreditation, has to admit that it has drawn us closer and closer to worldly education. Indeed, has led us to a remarkable compromise of standards and the infiltration of serious heretical teachings into many of our institutions.

The experience of Colin in the accreditation situation is that it is well-nigh impossible for this not to take place. Let us look at some of the hazards:

1. **Time**—Accrediting organizations call for extensive self-studies prior to the visitation of an accreditation team. It is true that every institution will be seeking an ongoing evaluation of its program and the meeting of its goals; but, here we have an outside organization dictating what is tantamount to thousands of hours of faculty time, over a period of two years in readying the institution for an accreditation visit. Such a procedure places inordinate burden and expense upon the institution.

2. **Resources**—No matter how favorable the accreditation, or the certification report is, there will always be a significant dollar amount that will be required to meet standards that are often inconsequential to the quality of education that is offered. For example, in three certification visits, in which Colin was president of Columbia Union College, there were requirements for an additional teacher in each area which the college could not afford and of placing material in the library amounting to a total of nearly $20,000—material which would probably be rarely read by any of the students or staff.

3. **Programming**—Accreditation does affect programming. For example, one of the visiting teams, in respect to education in its preliminary report, required that the dance be put into the physical education program. When it was pointed out that this was inimical to the goals of the institution, the final report called for the inclusion of rhythm; but here was an eroding of the purposes of the physical education program. Colin did not permit this part of the report to be implemented.

4. Pressure from staff members—The accrediting teams form an opportunity for staff members to place pressure upon administration to get for themselves that which they want, irrespective of the resources available and the needs of other departments. This pressure certainly became true in Madison College, and perhaps is one of the reasons for its rapid decline when faculty complained concerning salary situations. These complaints became an issue of continuing accreditation with the Southern Association. Colin himself had a problem with one of his departments where the accreditation team was used to try to pressure the administration to allocate an inordinate amount of money for this department.

But the issues are much deeper than money. Accreditation accepts the rights of an outside body, which does not share the Christian principles and the God-given mission of the Adventist Church, to evaluate the education program. This fact leads to the potential conflict between the voice of God and the voice of man.

We have always said that Christ is the Master Teacher, and that God's principles are the principles that ought to be followed; that the Eden school is the paradigm for all other schools, and that the Bible and Spirit of Prophecy offer the true basis of authentic education.

In spite of their sincere efforts to understand, there is no way that a non-Adventist body can fully comprehend and give counsel that would be to the best advantage of the development of God's work. We have to listen to one voice, the voice of God. In principle, accreditation makes this almost impossible. There, of course, are hundreds of quality institutions in the United States that are not accredited. We may think of some of the learned institutions such as Harvard and Yale. It might immediately be stated that they are the standard, and they do not need accreditation. But there are other well-known institutions such as Bob Jones University in the Carolinas and more than 160 such institutions in California alone, many of which offer some of the highest quality of education. In the true sense, it is Adventist education which is the standard, and thus requires no worldly accreditation.

The issue resolves itself around whether we want to listen to the voice of God or whether we want the approval of those who have imbibed the wisdom of this world. In this situation there seems no reasonable basis for the Christian to compromise. Some have argued that nonaccreditation of an institution makes it impotent and useless as far as students are concerned. There are even those who wrongly conclude that a nonaccredited institution cannot offer diplomas and degrees. Indeed, the degree and the diploma are quite independent of whether the institution is accredited or not. There are others who feel that it is impossible for credits to be transferred from one institution to the other; but the experience of the authors is that every quality program will find many institutions, both denominational and nondenominational, that will accept those credits. This fact has certainly been borne out at both Hartland and Weimar colleges. Further, some have suggested that graduates from nonaccredited institutions could not proceed to graduate school; but, while Colin was Dean of Weimar College, each student who applied to graduate school was accepted, and that included acceptance into a state university. Further, it has been stated that such graduates would not find a place in denominational employ. That also has not proved true in the experience of the authors. In other words, God finds an answer to each of these situations. It is not that we are suggesting that the basis of accreditation or nonaccreditation should be postulated upon the issues that have been quoted above. On the other hand, they demonstrate that many of the false understandings of accreditation have led many to blindly move into a pathway which has, in our judgment, done much to erode the God-centered base of Christian education.

God is calling upon the Adventist Church to prepare a people for a unique work, which will take the gospel, in Pentecostal power, to every nation, kindred, tongue, and people. Only an education that is stripped entirely of worldly infiltration can prepare such a generation of young people. It is our conviction that accreditation has seriously compromised, and perhaps in many ways, derailed the purpose of Christian education.

1. White, *Counsels to Parents, Teachers, and Students,* pages 480, 481.
2. Ibid., page 480.
3. White, *Medical Ministry,* pages 61, 62.
4. Ibid., page 84.
5. White, *Fundamentals of Christian Education,* page 534.
6. Branson, W. H., Fall Council speech, October 30, 1935.
7. Ibid.
8. Ibid.
9. Ibid.
10. Ibid.
11. *Review and Herald,* September 20, 1934.

Chapter 27
Public Funding of
Christian Education

There was a time when Seventh-day Adventists stood staunchly against the public funding of education. When the authors were still residents in Australia in the early 1960s, much controversy existed concerning the funding of private education by government. The church took a very strong stand against what it publicly declared to be "this iniquitous double taxation." The authors remember a petition that was sent to the churches, which they signed and submitted to the New South Wales State Government, urging it not to yield to the pressure of the Catholic Church to provide funds for private education. However, eventually those funds were allocated out of the public treasury. Uunfortunately, we were quick to accept them also. This indicates that our opposition had been a weak preference rather than an impelling conviction.[1]

Indeed, all around the world the Adventist Church has accepted state funds. This fact has frequently placed the education of the church in jeopardy. In some cases, this has led to the complete takeover of education. It has been argued by some that the government will take them over anyway. This is less-likely, however, when not one cent of government funds has been accepted. There is no question that the one who provides the finances is also likely to be the one who wants increasing control in the education program. This is only right, for no good government would expend public money without due control. In many parts of the world we have faced great difficulty after allowing government subsidies for education. This problem includes many parts of Africa, the West Indies, and of the Pacific Islands, as well as Australia and the United States.

The significance of accepting state funds was felt by Colin when he was president of Columbia Union College. The board had resolutely decided not to take Maryland State grants. Shortly after that, in an effort to provide more attractive curricular offerings for the students, a number of new courses were initiated by the Academic Affairs Committee. Immediately the Maryland Board of Higher Education sought to stop the implementation of the program, but when it was pointed out that no state funds were being accepted by Columbia Union College, the board quickly withdrew its objection.

A similar experience occurred in our educational system a number of decades ago in Fiji. Then the president of the West Fiji Mission, Pastor J. B. Keith, immediately reversed the situation of the acceptance of state funds, and was able to save the direction of our educational system there. It will be recalled also that years ago when the state took over nongovernmental schools in Sri Lanka, the Seventh-day Adventist schools were allowed to remain because they had not accepted funds. The situation was altogether different in certain nations of Africa where state funds were accepted. We now have lost control of our schools. In other nations, such as Grenada and Trinidad in the West Indies, we have found it difficult to dismiss teachers and principals who have been either apostate or immoral in their behavior. In Malaysia, after accepting government funds, the Adventist school in Kuala Lumpur was forbidden to teach Bible. The school soon closed because it no longer had a valid purpose.

There are many other hazards associated with the acceptance of state funds. Such a policy has a profound effect upon our believers to the point where they do not see, to the same extent, their God-given responsibility in the support of Christian education. Back in the 1960s, it was pointed out by the authors that should state funds be accepted, it would lead to much greater indebtedness by the denomination. It is not easy to indicate how this takes place, for it would seem that the reverse would be the case; but the experience in both Australia and North America has been that, indeed, there has been increased crippling debt in our institutions, since the acceptance of state funds. Maybe, as a result, the Lord allows us to pay the consequences of leaning upon the arm of flesh rather than upon the arm of the Spirit. At the end of the 1960s, the division subsidy remained constant at $25,000 per year for the operation of Avondale College. Today a very large amount of money is needed to subsidize the college, way out of proportion to the increase of inflation rate that has existed since that time. This increase in funding occurs, in spite of the fact that large sums of money are coming from government sources. Some argue that it would be wrong to deprive our young people of a Christian education because they could not afford it, except by the acceptance of government subsidies. This argument seems very difficult to combat. Yet, in those colleges where state funds have not been accepted, the authors have found that there have always been sufficient funds from private sources to help such individuals. Those who genuinely seek the Lord for their financial strength will unquestionably be provided with their needs.

One of the greatest problems confronting Seventh-day Adventist higher education in North America is the huge sums of money that have been accepted, either directly or indirectly, through student grants and loans. When these funds have begun to erode, the colleges have been left in dire financial difficulty because fewer and fewer students have been able to attend; and, therefore, the economy of the school has suffered dramatically. But there are other considerations. The acceptance of even indirect government aid through student loans and grants places the school under every federal educational ordinance. For example, Adventist schools have had to face Title IX, which deals with sex discrimination. Title VI deals with discrimination against the handicapped and the Buckley nondiscrimination amendment.[2] It is not that Seventh-day Adventists want to discriminate against the handicapped, nor, indeed, hide the records of students. The thought of government interference in these areas—the fact that special application has to be made to retain the Christian philosophy of the distinction between the sexes, and the right of colleges to continue to work with parents in the fuller education of their children—are areas which should be unacceptable to Christian educators. It is interesting to note that in North America, as in Australia, the financial security of the colleges has deteriorated subsequently to the acceptance of state-aid provisions.

Some have argued that Ellen White was in favor of the acceptance of government funds, on the basis of her experience with Malamulo in Africa. It will be recalled that Elder S. N. Haskell had been granted by Cecil Rhodes, then Premier of the Cape Colony, a large tract of land, in what later became Rhodesia and is now Zimbabwe, for the establishment of a school. Immediately the General Conference voted against acceptance of this property and asked Elder Haskell to return it. Haskell was devastated and wrote to Ellen White in Australia. He pointed out that this was not a government grant, for at that time "Rhodesia" was operated, independently of the British Government, by the British East Africa Company. Sister White agreed and strongly condemned the action of the General Conference. It is important to note that the basis upon which Haskell successfully argued his case with Ellen White was the fact that this was not a government grant, but was given by a private chartered company; and, therefore, it could not come under the restriction of the counsel not to be tied by a shoestring to the world.

A number of times we have been told that there are sufficient funds within the church to provide for our needs. We are given counsel as to what to do if we need to borrow. While borrowing should be avoided as far as possible, if it is necessary it would appear that we should not borrow from worldly institutions.

> In the establishment of training schools for workers, and especially in new fields where the brethren are few and their means limited, rather than delay the work it may be better to hire some money from the friends of the enterprise; but whenever it is possible, let our institutions be dedicated free from debt.

> The Lord has means for His work in the hands of His stewards; and as long as our schools have debts which were incurred in their establishment, in the erection of necessary buildings, and in providing necessary facilities, it is our duty to present the case to our brethren and ask them to lessen these debts. Our ministers should feel a burden for this work. [3]

To facilitate the finances of our schools, there are a number of other principles that should be applied. We should exercise the strictest financial measures.

> In the erection of school buildings, in their furnishing, and in every feature of their management the strictest economy must be practiced. [4]

Hopefully, while providing the strictest economy, we should, however, charge sufficient tuition to cover all the operating expenses of the college.

> In some of our schools the price of tuitions has been too low. This has in many ways been detrimental to the educational work.

It has brought discouraging debt; it has thrown upon the management a continual suspicion of miscalculation, want of economy, and wrong planning; it has been very discouraging to the teachers; and it leads the people to demand corresponding low prices in other schools. Whatever may have been the object in placing the tuition at less than a living rate, the fact that a school has been running behind heavily is sufficient reason for reconsidering the plans and arranging its charges so that in the future its showing may be different. The amount charged for tuition, board, and residence should be sufficient to pay the salaries of the faculty, to supply the table with an abundance of healthful, nourishing food, to maintain the furnishing of the rooms, to keep the buildings in repair, and to meet other necessary running expenses.[5]

It can be argued today that it can hardly be said that the cost of tuition is too low; indeed, all would agree that it is too high. If we follow the counsel of the Lord, however, in reducing the costs by the finest measures of economy, if we establish profit-producing industries in a quality work-education program, there would be reason to believe that the cost of education would be significantly less than it is today in our colleges. Above all, in considering the financing of our institutions, it is important for us to follow God's principles, and to lean upon Him for the provisions that are needed.

1. One worker, explaining his changed attitude to the acceptance of state-aid, summed up the situation, "It was easy to reject when it wasn't offered."
2. Briefly Title IX does not allow discrimination of sexes in dress, behavior, accommodation, or rules. Title VI requires expensive remodeling for handicapped students, whether there are such in attendance or not. The Buckley Amendment allows no communication with parents of college students on financial, citizenship, and academic performance without written consent of the student.
3. White, *Testimonies for the Church*, Volume 6, page 207.
4. Ibid., page 208.
5. Ibid., pages 210, 211.

Chapter 28

Academic Freedom in the Adventist School System

Modern concepts of academic freedom are cradled in the problems confronted by teachers, in the emergence of the modern universities during the Middle Ages. Some of the embryonic universities in Italy, such as the one at Bologna, placed inordinate restrictions upon teachers who could be fined for "cutting" a lecture, for lateness, for attracting too small an audience, for omissions and for avoiding the elucidation of difficult subjects.[1]

> At Bologna. . . the gilds [sic], which were the university, were organizations of the students, and the masters were hardly more than the hired men of the students, by whom they were subject to a rigid and detailed academic discipline.[2]

This state of affairs led many professors to seek positions in the northern universities, such as Paris, Oxford, and Cambridge, where the teachers were unquestionably in charge of the university administration and, to a large extent, the course curricula. Yet, even in these universities, the church was to wield great influence on both the direction and content of university courses; and, thus, the church was to be increasingly seen as the enemy of academic freedom by at least some academicians. While the universities arose independent of both church and state authorities and had freedoms known only to the clergy in Western Europe, church authority and discipline were exercised from time to time when teachers were held to have moved too far from ecclesiastical orthodoxy. In fact, at about the time of the rise of modern universities, Peter Ebelard[3] was placed under severe church discipline because of the skepticism perceived in his book, *Sic et Non*.[4]

The modern struggle for academic freedom has always been complex. In the United States, colleges may be divided in three broad categories:

1. State or county administered and funded
2. Privately administered but at least partially state funded
3. Privately administered and funded

Each of these represents educational approaches which have clear implications for academic freedom. While it is understood that state and county schools have no right to support a specific religious stream of thought, there can always arise questions as to how free the teacher is to press concepts which might be seen to subvert the state and/or the nation. On the other hand, private schools frequently have well-defined religious goals which do not allow for unlimited or even wide-ranging differences of content by its teachers. This policy certainly was true of most of the early universities and colleges which were established in the United States, although not as clearly today in institutions that are operated by conservative and biblically-based churches. Obviously, there can be some tension when operating, or sponsoring, organizations seek to exercise what they consider to be their right to limit the parameters, or content emphasis, of teachers. This situation may be further complicated when such institutions are the recipients of large sums of public moneys.

The church/state issue is most relevant in such situations; for those who vigorously support the concept of separation of church and state see grave constitutional dangers in providing public funds to support institutions clearly espousing specific religious points of view. Indeed, the survival of some colleges has eventually been contingent upon revamping curricula and courses, so that they are electic enough to no longer be distinguished as supporting any specific religious group.

This procedure raises an issue that's sometimes overlooked in the concepts of academic freedom. Whereas most studies addressing the issue tend to focus upon the teacher's right to teach according to his professional understandings and convictions; less is said about the freedom of the operating organization to preserve its rights to maintain the integrity of the purpose for which the institution was founded. This issue of fundamental rights is frequently the basis of disagreement, if not serious tension, between faculty and boards. The issue is seriously complicated when public funds are provided to the institution. it is the writers' conviction that the rights of sponsoring organizations are greatly eroded when such moneys are accepted.

What really then is academic freedom? Most definitions center upon the maintenance of the rights of teachers to pursue and teach truth as they see it. For example, W. T. Couch defines it as follows:

> Academic freedom is the principle designed to protect the teacher from hazards that tend to prevent him from meeting his obligations in the pursuit of truth.[5]

Such definitions present serious problems and questions to the Seventh-day Adventist Church. It is held that truth resides in, or is at least always consistent with, the revealed Word of God; and, that, in the fullest sense, truth resides in a Person—Jesus Christ. This concept immediately defines limits for the pursuit of truth. The search for that which is clearly inconsistent with the teachings of Christ is perceived as a pursuit of error rather than truth. Couch's definition, as it is presented without limitations, becomes wholly existentialist, for the definition of truth is left to reside in the mind of each teacher. Couch also fails to address the most pressing issue—whether the teacher has the right to indoctrinate the youth with his ideas of truth.

If academic freedom presupposes the unlimited right of teachers to indoctrinate students with their concepts of truth, it is obvious that much error will be presented. The issue, of course, is delicate and complex. Much evidence exists to show that both church and state have been responsible for the perpetration of grave errors, by repressive measure, and restrictions upon academic freedom; on the other hand, it is just as demonstrable that the exercising of academic freedom by certain teachers has led to the propounding of gross and grave error. Therefore, it should not be urged that academic freedom is necessary for the pursuit of truth. Rather, man requires a paradigm outside, and infinitely above, himself by which to evaluate and define truth. For Seventh-day Adventists this rule of faith is unquestionably the Word of God. Thus Ellen White has said:

> The Bible is not to be tested by men's ideas of science, but science is to be brought to the test of the unerring standard.[6]

In the ultimate analysis of modern concepts of academic freedom, it becomes clear that such testing is absolutely essential for the preservation and perpetration of error. The pursuit of error, rather than truth, demands a concept of academic freedom. In the Garden of Eden, Satan based his appeal to Eve on the basis that she would achieve a freedom yet unknown to her if she would accept the deceptive error that he propounded as truth. So today strong supporters have seen agitation for academic freedom as necessary for the toleration of error. For example:

> All justification for intellectual freedom rests upon a conception of the nature of truth which implies a reason for toleration of error.[7]

While for many this argument may be persuasive, Seventh-day Adventists have long held that there can be no toleration of error, making a clear distinction between the toleration of the one in error and the toleration of the error. Many lose much by failing to acknowledge or make this distinction.

Further, Metzger offers a rationale for academic freedom which is not built upon faith or truth in God and His Word; and, while many of the values are praiseworthy in themselves, they fail to be secured to a transcendent value system.

> Finally, the rationale for academic freedom has been endowed with certain fundamental values.... Such values as tolerance and honesty, publicity and testifiability, individuality and cooperativeness, have been part of the scientific bequest.[8]

There is another issue that's involved in the modern concepts of academic freedom which should be of more than passing concern to Seventh-day Adventists. This issue is the indisputable link with the development of evolutionary concepts of science. While acknowledging that there's nothing new under the sun, Metzger nevertheless concludes,

> A "new" rationale of academic freedom grew out of Darwinian debate.[9]

He further concludes,

> Science invested the theory of academic freedom with a special conception of truth and a formula for tolerating error.... Without the canons of evolutionary science, we contend, the modern rationale of academic freedom would not exist.[10]

If Metzger is right, and the evidence supports him, the relationship between the toleration of error and the concepts of academic freedom is confirmed. The conservatism of Adventist education is considered oppressive by those, including Metzger, who favor the so-called "academic freedom" and error in the educational program that results from evolution. One of the most persistent attacks upon Seventh-day Adventist colleges is that they are resistant to change; and, therefore, they are repressing the legitimate search for truth. It is our observation that such charges are substantially false. These changes often result from confusion between the church's God-given role to preserve and defend truth and claims that the church is stifling the search for truth. There is significant evidence that those who have been successful in eroding the bases of truth in Seventh-day Adventist institutions present themselves as liberals and crusaders for individual rights. There is far less evidence that such people extend these freedom principles to those of basic Adventist persuasion once they are in position of authority. Once error is established, it has never existed long without intolerance of not only truth but also of those who stand upon a platform of truth.

> If anything, it is the liberal and humanistic institutions, with their pose of tolerance and sweet reasonableness, that are the most dangerous.[11]

Christian educators and administrators of Christian institutions face a constant pressure to erode truth and standards, all in the name of academic and personal freedom. Such efforts ignore Christ's declaration that

The truth shall make you free (John 8:32).

The false basis of most freedom cries can be seen by the erosion of truth as observed in early Christian schools, Reformational schools, and now in Seventh-day Adventist schools. The freedom cries are based upon the fundamental error that it is the reverse—freedom will lead to truth.

A few years ago, General conference leadership sought to establish a statement of faith in the areas of creationism, inspiration, and revelation. The reaction of many Seventh-day Adventist academies was strong and immediate. Many saw in these statements the potential to erode their rights and freedoms as academicians. This reaction has triggered the issue of academic freedom to be aired by faculties and in classrooms, at a level previously unknown in Seventh-day Adventist circles. Some academicians have banded together, determined to resist all efforts to confine their teachings to a certain body of orthodoxy, or to place parameters upon their interpretations in any area that impinges upon their disciplines.

In the light of some of the historical bases behind the movement for academic freedom, it is pertinent to discuss the impact of demands for academic freedom in Seventh-day Adventist education. Some of the questions Seventh-day Adventists need to address are the following:

1. Do teachers in Adventist colleges have the right to freedom, to follow their consciences and beliefs in what they teach?

2. Does the church have the right, indeed, the responsibility, to monitor what is being taught in the colleges that it sponsors?

3. Should the church exercise authority to ensure that only that which is consistent with its articles of faith is taught in its colleges?

4. What rights do parents and students have to expect orthodoxy from their teachers?

5. Do lay church members have rights to require accountability of teachers in Adventist colleges and schools?

These questions raise some critical, ethical, and moral issues which cannot be allowed to go unanswered. First, it should be observed that teachers are potentially the most powerful people in the Adventist Church. They have, as their students, predominantly young people at an age when the new, the controversial, and the novel are appealing. Yet, rarely do these youth have the experience to adequately evaluate the concepts their teachers are presenting. The teacher also has had time to finely hone his arguments, while many students have little such background. Further, the teacher, as the students' examiner, holds a powerful hand over the destiny of the students. One is highly motivated to uncritically accept the words of his professors, and to regurgitate them in examinations that are prepared and marked by these professors.

It can never be denied that each teacher must be allowed the freedom to follow his own conscience, but this freedom does not, as some have assumed, give the teacher the right to urge his convictions upon others. There is a strong ethical issue at stake because the students are a captive audience. It is not ethical to subject these impressionable youths to viewpoints that are different from those for which the college that they have chosen to attend purports to stand. Unfortunately, many professors have stooped to this unethical conduct, thus misusing their claims of academic freedom.

Seventh-day Adventist colleges and schools are hardly eclectic institutions. Like other church-based colleges, they have been established to teach every discipline centered upon the Bible and consistent with the beliefs of the Adventist Church; thus, there is no reasonable argument for the normal concepts of academic freedom. Such concepts are inimical to the very purposes for which Seventh-day Adventist colleges have been established—to teach and preserve the beliefs of the church. All teachers have an undeniable responsibility and obligation to teach consistently with these beliefs. This is not to suggest that teachers should be dishonest to their own convictions; on the contrary, absolute honesty would demand that teachers with different beliefs should not apply for teaching positions in Adventist institutions. They should withdraw once they are unable to teach consistently with Adventist beliefs. It is not sufficient to refrain from teaching that which is inconsistent with Adventist theology. The teacher should be able, in conscience, to teach and practice that which is consistent with these church beliefs. Academic freedom in an Adventist college can only mean freedom to teach within the parameters of the fundamental beliefs of the Adventist Church.

Church leaders and laity alike have a most sacred responsibility to preserve the integrity of our colleges. It should be noted that educational institutions have played a significant role in the deviation of most God-centered movements, e.g., the Jews, the early Christians, and the Protestants. While it is first the teacher's responsibility to decide whether his teaching is consistent with church beliefs, realistically not all will have the integrity to make this decision. The church has the obligation to ensure this integrity, even if it means the dismissal of a faculty member or administrator. The rights movements of the last three decades have tended to overlook the rights of institutions, but the integrity of God's church is of prime importance. It may immediately be argued that such measures will be oppressive, and will not provide a climate for open and honest inquiry. There is ample opportunity within the Adventist Church for wide-ranging inquiry, but the landmarks are unchallengeable. This statement does not mean that the landmarks cannot be studied, and that earnest effort should not be extended to gain fuller insights into their meaning and relevance to personal living. But the essential features of these great truths, established by prayer, study, and revelation, are irremovable.

Unfortunately, many teachers have been seriously affected by their study in non-Adventist institutions; and this experience has weakened their faith in the Advent truth. Ellen White foresaw this dilemma and gave the definite answer to this problem:

> Those who seek the education that the world esteems so highly, are gradually led further and further from the principles of truth until they become educated worldlings. . . . They have chosen to accept what the world calls knowledge in the place of the truths which God has committed to men through His ministers and prophets and apostles. And there are some who, having secured this worldly education, think that they can introduce it into our schools. But let me tell you that you must not take what the world calls higher education and bring it into our schools and sanitariums and churches. We need to understand these things. I speak to you definitely. This must not be done.[12]

At its root, the call for academic freedom is primarily motivated by self-interest rather than love for God's church, His Word, and the youth studying in Adventist institutions. The church must directly address the issue because the fundamental teachings and beliefs of the Adventist Church will change, by default, if this is not done.

The cry for academic freedom is generated by those who would deny parents the freedom to have their children receive an education based upon the stated principles of the institution to which they have entrusted their children, and for which they have made many financial sacrifices. Many professors deny their students the freedom to learn Seventh-day Adventist principles that are untrammeled by doubt and innuendo. They further deny the employing institution the right to pursue the aims that are inherent in its establishment. This is tyranny of the worst form, for it usurps a freedom for the professor at the expense of those who have a God-given right to exert it. Much of that which masquerades as academic freedom is, when unmasked, in very fact, academic coercion.

1. Knight, E. W., *Twenty Centuries of Education,* (Ginn and Co.), page 127.
2. Hofstadter, Richard, *Academic Freedom in the Age of the College,* (Columbia University Press, © 1969), page 4.
3. Paris, France, 1079–1142.
4. *Yes and No.*
5. Quoted in Kirk, Russell, *Academic Freedom,* (Henry Regency Co., © 1955), page 1.
6. White, *Counsels to Parents, Teachers, and Students,* page 425.

7. Metzger, Walter P., *Academic Freedom in the Age of the University,* (Columbia University Press, © 1969), page 90.
8. Ibid., pages 91, 92.
9. Ibid., page 89.
10. Ibid.
11. Hook, Sidney, *Academic Freedom and Academic Anarchy,* (Cowles Book Co., Inc., New York, © 1970), page 79.
12. White, *Fundamentals of Christian Education,* pages 535, 536.

Chapter 29
The Education
of the Redeemed

As boys, we somehow shared the misconception that the redeemed would instantly receive infinite knowledge and wisdom. This idea, of course, was a serious misconception. Only God is omniscient.[1] However, eternity will provide an ongoing education. This education will not consist of hypotheses and theories, but the pure truth that Christ, the Master Teacher, will present to the saints. Constantly they will receive ever-increasing knowledge of the character of God and of the works of His creation. With increasing wisdom, the saints will more fully glorify their Lord and mature in the reflection of His character. The perfect education of Eden will continue in the earth made new.

Through the ministry of the angels, the redeemed will learn more fully of guidance and protection that has been afforded them by the Divine.

> Every redeemed one will understand the ministry of angels in his own life. The angel who was his guardian from his earliest moment; the angel who watched his steps, and covered his head in the day of peril; the angel who was with him in the valley of the shadow of death, who marked his resting place, who was the first to greet him in the resurrection morning—what will it be to hold converse with him, and to learn the history of divine interposition in the individual life, of heavenly cooperation in every work for humanity![2]

It will be expected that the saints will receive a balanced work-study-outreach program; and, indeed, this is the case. The education upon this earth is but a preparation for the education of the new earth; and, therefore, it is logical that all three aspects of education will be in the education of the saints, before and after the second coming of Jesus.

The prophet, Isaiah, clearly indicates, at least in part, the nature of the work-education program.

> They shall build houses, and inhabit them; and they shall plant vineyards, and eat the fruit of them. They shall not build, and another inhabit; they shall not plant, and another eat: for as the days of a tree are the days of my people, and mine elect shall long enjoy the work of their hands (Isaiah 65:21, 22).

The academic program will indeed be a challenging one of considerable variety.

> There will be open to the student, history of infinite scope and of wealth inexpressible. Here, from the vantage ground of God's word, the student is afforded a view of the vast field of history and may gain some knowledge of the principles that govern the course of human events. But his vision is still clouded, and his knowledge incomplete. Not until he stands in the light of eternity will he see all things clearly.

> Then will be opened before him the course of the great conflict that had its birth before time began, and that ends only when time shall cease. The history of the inception of sin; of fatal falsehood in its crooked working; of truth that, swerving not from its own straight lines, has met and conquered over all will be made manifest. The veil that interposes between the visible and the invisible world will be drawn aside, and wonderful things will be revealed. [3]

> There will be music there, and song, such music and song as, save in the visions of God, no mortal ear has heard or mind conceived. . . .

> All the treasures of the universe will be open to the study of God's children. With unutterable delight we shall enter into the joy and wisdom of unfallen beings. We shall share the treasures gained through ages upon ages spent in contemplation of God's handiwork. And the years of eternity, as they roll, will continue to bring more glorious revelations. [4]

No worthwhile study will be denied the inhabitants of the new earth. Some may ask the purpose of an outreach program in the new earth. Surely this ministry has been necessary this side of eternity, that man might be invited into the family of God. Yet, there will be a valid outreach for the saints. They will play a critical role in sharing the evidence of God's love to all unfallen beings. As God continues His creation, it will be the privilege of the saints to witness to the new beings. This witness will play a significant role in the assurance that

> Affliction shall not rise up the second time (Nahum 1:9).

In many ways, the education of the new earth will parallel that of the Eden school; but, in a number of ways, there will be differences.

> Not all the conditions of that first school of Eden will be found in the school of the future life. No tree of knowledge of good and evil will afford opportunity for temptation. No tempter is there, no possibility of wrong. Every character has withstood the testing of evil, and none are longer susceptible to its power.[5]

We have the privilege now to experience for ourselves and our children the same educational principles that it will be our joy to experience throughout history.

> The life on earth is the beginning of the life in heaven; education on earth is an initiation into the principles of heaven; the lifework here is a training for the lifework there. What we now are, in character and holy service, is the sure foreshadowing of what we shall be.[6]

It is not possible to honor God by an education that is defective, even in one principle of His kingdom. It is not possible to prepare youths who are so totally committed to Christ that they will possess the characters that are necessary to vindicate their God, unless our education is unflawed. It is not possible for Jesus to return until our education reflects the principles of redemption. How much is at stake only eternity will reveal. God's call for educational reformation will be heeded by those who love the Lord and long for His coming. Because man has failed God in every Christ-centered educational program of the past, the work of God has been delayed.

The end of sin and suffering is in the hands of God's people. It wasn't the wickedness of the Canaanites that delayed the Israelites' entry into the Promised Land. It was the faithlessness of the Israelites. So, too, the return of the Saviour is not delayed by the wickedness of the world, tragic as this is, but by the neglect and faithlessness of God's church to rise up and follow Him, free of human modification. It is the prayer of the authors that we will put aside our rebellion against God's plan of education, that we will follow His counsel implicitly, thus becoming the first generation in the history of the world to fully unite education with redemption. Then, quickly, a Spirit-filled generation will arise. The gospel will be given with Pentecostal power to every corner of the earth. All humans will make an irrevocable decision for or against God. Probation will close, and Jesus will return to usher in the Kingdom of Righteousness. What joy awaits the trusting saints!

1. Having infinite knowledge.
2. White, *Education.*, page 305.
3. Ibid., page 304.
4. Ibid., page 307.
5. Ibid., page 302.
6. Ibid., page 307.

Chapter 30
Biography

Colin and Russell Standish first experienced Christian education in fifth grade when a change in the location of their home permitted them to attend the Newcastle Seventh-day Adventist School (Australia) in January 1943. Although that school, which encompassed all grades of primary and high school, possessed fewer than fifty pupils, they were successful in the New South Wales government matriculation examinations in 1949. The school could have doubled the enrollment had all Seventh-day Adventist members sent their children to the church school. However a number of parents estimated that the educational standards of the government high schools were superior; thus they elected to send their children to those schools. But, the parents of the authors placed a high value upon Christian education; and, while finding difficulty in meeting the fees, sacrificed for the sake of their conviction wishing the very best for their sons.

Upon leaving school, both enrolled in the primary teaching training course at Avondale College. In 1951, they completed the two-year certificate course. They were then barely 18 years of age, and were appointed to one-teacher primary (elementary) schools in rural areas of New South Wales. Colin taught for two years in Burringbar and one year at Mullumbimby, on the far north coast of New South Wales. Russell was appointed to Mumblepeg, in the sheep and wheat district of western New South Wales. After one year there, he transferred to Albury on the New South Wales–Victorian border for two years.

Completing three years, each, of primary-school teaching, they both decided that they wished to study to become high-school teachers. With this goal in view, they commenced studies at Sydney University, completing a major in history and undertaking an honors degree in psychology. The field of study, which required both a theoretical and an empirical thesis, was in the area of learning theory. Colin continued in this area, obtaining his Master of Arts degree with honors in 1961, and completed his Doctor of Philosophy in 1964. In 1967, he completed the Masters degree in Education. All these qualifications were completed at the University of Sydney. Russell subsequently studied medicine, graduating as a physician in 1964. In 1970, he became a member of the Royal College of Physicians (U.K.). In 1983, he was a fellow of the Royal Colleges of Physicians in Edinburgh and Glasgow.

In 1965, Colin was appointed Chairman of the Department of Education at Avondale College. Also he has held the post of academic dean in West Indies College (1970), president of West Indies College (1970–73), chairman of the Department of Psychology, Columbia Union College (1974), president of Columbia Union College (1974–78), dean of Weimar College (1978–83), and is currently president of Hartland Institute in Virginia.

While working in administrative roles in denominational colleges for 14 years in Australia, Jamaica, and the United States, Colin gained valuable insights into current Seventh-day Adventist educational institutions. While noting some strengths, he came to the conclusion that they had been greatly infiltrated by worldly educational philosophies and practices.

When given the opportunity to establish the Christian college at Weimar Institute in 1978, he enthusiastically accepted the post. He had taught the principles of Christian education in each of the colleges where he served, and saw Weimar College as a challenge, where the validity of the principles of Christian education for modern times could be demonstrated. There a program of academic excellence was combined with the truly Seventh-day Adventist principles of a work program, in which students learned specific skills and an outreach ministry.

In 1983 Colin was invited to become the foundational president of Hartland Institute, the goals of which are to educate young people to selflessly offer their lives in service for God and man. The college's training is enhanced by the ministry of the wellness center, publishing house, and world mission divisions.

Russell's service has taken him away from education, but his intense interest in it has been maintained. He has been associated with the schools of nursing at Bangkok Adventist Hospital (Thailand) and Sydney Adventist Hospital (Australia). He also lectured at the University of Sydney for five years. Russell spent 31½ years in denominational service, first as a teacher and later as a medical missionary. He is presently the editor of the *Remnant Herald* and speaker for Remnant Ministries, headquartered in Melbourne, Australia.

Russell has also served on the boards of a number of Seventh-day Adventist educational institutions. Both authors are dedicated to the scriptural and Spirit of Prophecy principles of education, perceiving these to be inestimably superior to those of the most prestigious secular institutions. Nothing is more important, in their view, than the preparation of young people for this life and for the life to come.